From VBA to VSTO

Is Excel's New Engine for You?

Dr. Gerard M. Verschuuren

Holy Macro! Books

Written by:
Dr. Gerard M. Verschuuren

Edited by:
Linda DeLonais

On the Cover:
Design by Shannon Mattiza, 6'4 Productions.

Publisher:
Bill Jelen

Associate Publisher:
Lora White

Published by:
Holy Macro! Books
PO Box 82
Uniontown, Ohio, USA 44685

Distributed by:
Independent Publishers Group

First printing:
April 2006.
Printed in the United States of America

Library of Congress Data
From VBA to VSTO: Is Excel's New Engine for You? / Dr. Gerard M. Verschuuren
Library of Congress Control Number: 2006924353

ISBN: 1-932802-14-2

Table of Contents

About the Author

Dr. Gerard M. Verschuuren is a *Microsoft Certified Professional* specialized in VB, VBA, and VB.NET. He has more than 20 years of experience in teaching at colleges and corporations.

He holds Master's degrees in Biology (Human Genetics) and in Philosophy, plus a Doctorate in the Philosophy of Science from Universities in Europe.

He is the author of several books, including:

> ➤ Excel for Scientists and Engineers (2005, Holy Macro Books)

> ➤ Life Scientists, Their Convictions, Their Activities, and Their Values (1995, Genesis Publishing Company)

He is also the author behind the **Visual Learning Series** (MrExcel.com):

> ➤ Slide Your Way Through Excel VBA (2003)

> ➤ Join the Excellers League (2004)

> ➤ Your Access to the World (2004)

> ➤ Master the Web (2005)

> ➤ Access VBA Made Accessible (2005)

Prologue

This book is for those who wonder whether they should transit from Excel/VBA to Excel/VSTO. It was not written for people who want to learn programming in Excel, nor was it written for those (professional) developers who want to know all the ins and outs of VSTO programming.

My only intention is to help VBA users to make the right decision as to whether they should transit to VSTO and, if they decide to do so, to be aware of the hurdles they have to leap and the benefits they will reap.

Therefore, in this book I focus on the differences between both programming languages by explaining where they diverge and by showing examples of code on both sides of the transition line.

By using so-called Rosetta stones, I show you, using some carefully selected examples, where the two languages differ.

My hope is that this book will be a helpful guide in making a well-balanced decision in this matter and, if you do venture the transition, that it will smooth the process that lies ahead of you.

gmv

P.S. When writing this book, I had to use the Beta 2 version of Visual Studio 2005. Later releases may have some adaptations not mentioned in this book.

Listing of Code Samples

1   Visual Studio Tools for Office

1.1   Why VSTO?

VSTO stands for *Visual Studio Tools for Office* and is sometimes pronounced as "Visto." VSTO is an alternative to VBA, and will most likely replace VBA in time. I assume that you already know VBA for Excel. If not, study the interactive visual learning CD "Slide Your Way Through Excel VBA" (available from www.mrexcel.com or www.amazon.com).

You probably have been working with VBA for quite a while and like working with this programming tool. Why switch to something new? You may not need to switch soon, but it looks like Microsoft is going to discontinue VBA in its new releases from 2008 on. At some point in time, you may have to transit to VSTO – unless you want to stay with older versions of Excel and related Office products.

So the question is: Why is Microsoft so excited about VSTO? Is it just because it is a new product? I don't think so. The answer has something to do with the evolution of another product: Visual Basic, in particular *VB 6.0*. *VB 6.0* is an application on its own that allows you to create your own new applications – simple applications or fancier applications similar to Excel – by using the Visual Basic programming language. *VB 6.0* uses Visual Basic in much the same way that Excel uses Visual Basic in VBA.

Visual Basic is a powerful programming language, but there are other languages such as C++ (pronounced "C-plus-plus"), Java, and so forth. Professional developers are usually specialized in one of these languages, and if they don't speak Visual Basic, they cannot use *VB 6.0*.

To alleviate this problem, Microsoft came up with a new development tool, called *Visual Studio .NET* (pronounced "Dot-net"). The VS.NET version not only uses the programming language Visual Basic, but also other languages such as C++, C# (pronounced "C-sharp"), and J#. In addition, it has many other advantages that we will discuss later. In this book, I will just focus on the Visual Basic language of .NET, which is referred to as VB.NET.

Table 1 Programming languages vs. development tools	Tool	VBA	VB 6.0	VSTO	VS.NET
	Language(s)	VB		VB.NET, C#, C++, J#	

Can you use VB.NET to program existing applications such as Excel? Can you use the power of Excel, as exemplified in its graphs, in VB.NET? Yes, you can, but the process is involved and not very efficient. So, Microsoft came up with a new engine: *Visual Studio Tools for Office* (or VSTO). VSTO is basically a *Visual Studio* add-in.

Sorry if the terminology has become too mystifying and confusing. From now on, I will call the "old" tool VBA, and the "new" tool VSTO. VBA works with the "old" language – VB – whereas VSTO works with the "new" language – VB.NET.

Table 2

Time lines for VBA, VSTO, and VB 6.0

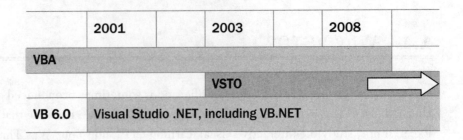

	2001	2003	2008
VBA			
		VSTO	
VB 6.0	Visual Studio .NET, including VB.NET		

1.2   The New Tool: VSTO

VSTO works within the *Visual Studio .NET* environment, also called the *.NET Framework*. VSTO interacts directly with Office applications such as Excel – and that's why you should know about it, and in time may even have to know about it. Let us summarize some of the big advantages VSTO has over VBA:

- ➤ Works with your favorite language: VB, C^{++}, etc.
- ➤ Uses more powerful forms with expanded potential.
- ➤ Improves access to data residing on a server (SQL and ADO).
- ➤ Enhances communication with Web Servers.
- ➤ Protects users with better security.
- ➤ Protects code by hiding it from view and preventing inadvertent, inept changes.
- ➤ Improves the way you deploy new code and future updates to other users.

All of these issues will receive due attention in the next chapters. Don't feel overwhelmed by the terminology at this point. The key issue remains: How do you create the new code? That will be our main concern.

Before we go into code issues, I want to address another point: Where is the new code going to reside? The code you create for Excel in VSTO is not located inside the document (as it is with VBA), but rather it is a separate DLL file (*Dynamic-Link-Library*). The Excel document has been given properties that contain "directions" to a certain DLL file at a certain location. The *.dll* file is called an assembly.

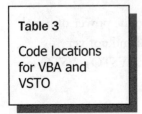

Table 3

Code locations for VBA and VSTO

VBA		VSTO	
.XLS file	VBA code	.XLS file	.DDL file from VSTO

Because VSTO code is built as a *.dll* file, this code file can be located anywhere. If the code is associated with a particular Workbook used by a single user, you can store it together with the document on that user's hard disk. But you can also store the file separately on a network where it can then be downloaded by each user the first time the Workbook is opened. Other possible locations are a corporate intranet or a secured internet site.

Table 4 .XLS and .DLS file origins and links	The new situation		
	.XLS file Made in Excel	.XLS file is "linked" to .DLL file	.DLL file Made in VSTO

How is it possible for VSTO to interact with Excel and other Office applications? Thanks to PIAs (*Primary Interop Assemblies*). PIAs allow VB.NET code to call Excel code, but they must be explicitly or manually installed with Office 2003+ by including the ".NET programmability support" option for each Office product during or after the installation process (see 12.1).

1.3   The New Language: VB.NET

How does VB.NET as it is used in VSTO differ from VB as used in VBA? We won't go into details yet, but the main difference is that the syntax or grammar of the VB.NET language is much more consistent, strict, and logical than what you are used to in the VBA version. I just want to mention a few inconsistencies in VBA's VB language that perhaps have baffled you many times:

➤ Functions require parentheses, but methods reject them.

➤ Some data types can change type automatically, but others can't.

➤ Most properties have to be specified, but some don't (they're called default).

➤ Some indexes start at 0, others at 1.

➤ Some variables have to be initialized with the *Set* keyword, but not all.

As we will shortly see in greater detail, VB.NET is a much more streamlined language than VB. This is definitely an advantage for a "born" programmer, but it may be a bit of a problem when you want to transfer or migrate code from VBA (which is based on VB) into VSTO (which is based on VB.NET).

When creating new code from scratch in VSTO, you will have to get used to those stricter rules. One of them is that all type conversions have to be done explicitly for situations where there is no automatic conversion in VB.NET.

You may ask yourself whether this is worth the price. We report, you decide. Given the many advantages that come with VSTO, you may become convinced of its superiority. Given the fact that VSTO will replace VBA some day, you may not have a choice if – for whatever reason – you have to deal with upcoming versions of Excel.

Table 5

VSTO eliminates many of the inconsistencies that plague VBA

Some inconsistencies in VBA's Visual Basic				
Space after methods	MsgBox "Message"	⇔	Parentheses after functions	If MsgBox("Save?",vbYesNo) = vbYes Then
Automatic conversion	var = TextBox1.Text * TextBox2.Text	⇔	Required conversion	var = **Val**(TextBox1.Text) + **Val**(TextBox2.Text)
Property missing (default)	var = ActiveCell	⇔	Property required, not default	var = ActiveCell.**BackColor**
Index starts at 0	For i = **0** To ListBox1.ListIndex	⇔	Index starts at 1	For i = **1** To Sheets.Count
Value type without Set	var = ActiveCell	⇔	Reference type requires Set	**Set** var = ActiveSheet

2   Structure of the Tool (VSTO)

2.1   The .NET Framework

The *.NET Framework* is the backbone of VSTO. What is actually in the *.NET Framework*? Well, it is loaded with hundreds of classes and interfaces! Here are its main layers:

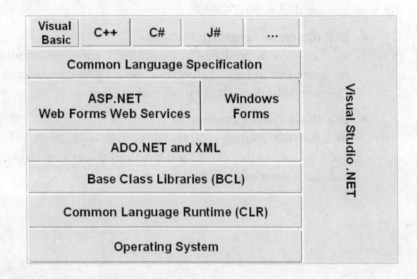

Figure 1

Illustration of the layers that comprise the .NET Framework

Table 6   Description of the layers that comprise the .NET Framework

VB.NET	One of the languages that you can use to write code in VSTO is *Visual Basic* – or more in particular, VB.NET (see 2.4).
ASP.NET Forms	There are Interfaces for *Windows Forms* (see 7.1), *Web Forms,* and *Web Services.* In order to use *Web Services*, you may have to install extra components (which we will not discuss here).
ADO.NET XML	In the background, much code is automatically converted into *XML* to deal with remote access, so you are off the hook yourself. You will find ADO.NET in 10.3.
BCL	BCL holds very powerful class libraries such as *System.Math, System.IO, System.Windows, System.Drawing,* and *System.Data.*
CLR	CLR takes care of memory use, common data types (see 5.1), security (see 12.1), garbage collection (see 11.3), and much more.

What are CLR and BCL? Perhaps you remember the VB Runtime in VB 6.0. It provided some very powerful services such as the following:

> **Automatic memory management:**
> Destroying objects and variables once they go out of scope

> **Safety checking on code:**
> For example, this prevents you from referencing an array outside its boundaries

> **Functions:**
> For things like string manipulation (*InStr*), user input (*MsgBox*), and type conversion (*CInt*)

Well, VB.NET has split these services into two separate entities, but they are much more comprehensive than before:

> **CLR (*Common Language Runtime*):**
> CLR reads code produced by the VB.NET compiler, scrutinizes it before execution, and cleans up unused variables and objects (so-called garbage collection; see 11.3). Code that runs under the control of the CLR is called "managed" code.

> **BCL (*Base Class Libraries*):**
> BCL provides many regular functions such as *MsgBox()*, *InStr()*, and *UCase()*. In addition, it contains many other classes and functions to perform data management and file management – and that's what most of this book about.

2.2   The Workspace (IDE)

A fancier name for the workspace is: *Integrated Development Environment*, or IDE. It has the following components, more or less different from VBA, and definitely more sophisticated:

Figure 2

Workspace components

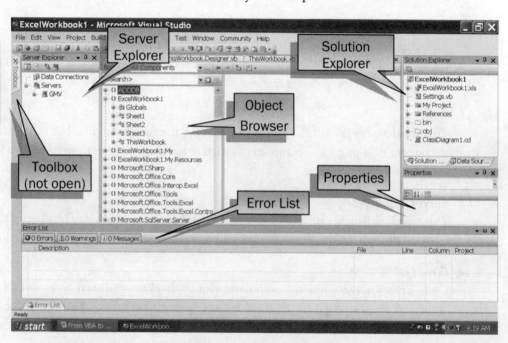

Window	How to Open Window
Solution Explorer:	*View → Solution Explorer*
Toolbox:	*View → Toolbox* (visible here, but docked at left)
Server Explorer:	*View → Server Explorer*
Error List:	*View → Error List*
Object Browser:	*View → Object Browser*
Properties:	*View → Properties* (empty here because no object has been selected)
One of the many windows not shown here is the Output Window	Use either *Debug → Windows → Output* or *View → Other Windows → Output*

Table 7

Accessing Workspace components

Solution Explorer:

A *Solution* can include one or more projects, in many different languages. The window can list general code modules, possibly one or more form modules, one or more class modules, plus a section called *References*. The last section lists the assemblies or components referenced by this particular *Solution*, so their classes become accessible for the developer. To add a new *Reference*, right-click this section (or choose *Project → Add References*).

Properties Window:

This window is very similar to the one in VBA. Changes to the properties in this window cause changes in the code. This code is usually written for you in files that you will only see if you open them from the *Solution Explorer*.

Toolbox:

This window is very similar to the one in VBA for *Form* controls, but it has many new tools and also stores non-graphical components such as database connections. That's why you see several categories in the toolbox.

Server Explorer:

This window lists Server components for database connections. The elements displayed can be dragged directly to the Form designer in order to create the proper connection (see 10.3).

Error List:

Code Errors detected by the automatic syntax checker are listed here. Double-clicking on an error takes you straight to the troublesome spot in your code. You can also use the line number of each error, but then you need all your code lines numbered: *Tools → Options → Text Editor → Basic →* ☑ *Line Numbers*.

Object Browser:

This window shows you all the available classes, just like VBA. But be aware that VSTO is much more class- and object-oriented than VBA. Literally everything is done through objects and the classes of which they are instances (see 3.1).

Immediate Window:

Debug.Print commands from VBA have been replaced with: *System.Diagnostics.Debug.Write("...")* statements. Their output is displayed in the Immediate Window. But there is more to this window (see 8.2).

Class View Window:

This window shows you a listing of all *References* (plus their sub-classes) and all objects in your project.

There are many more windows than we can discuss here.

You can have several windows available at the same time. If you click a Window's *pintag* icon that Window will dock on the side or bottom, thus hiding when the mouse is not hovering over it.

Figure 3

Windows docked at side and bottom of Workspace

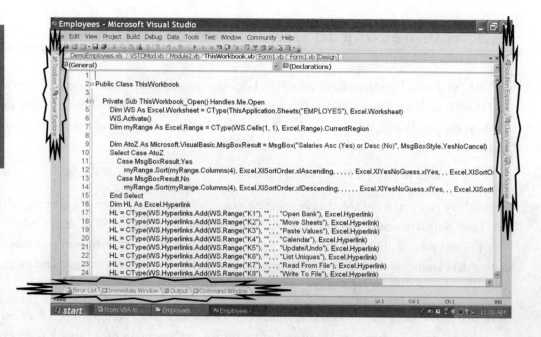

You also have the option of keeping several windows open at the same time by clicking their *pintag* icons again. However, some of these will be combined on the side with a set of tabs at the bottom.

Figure 4

Clicking its pintag opens a docked window

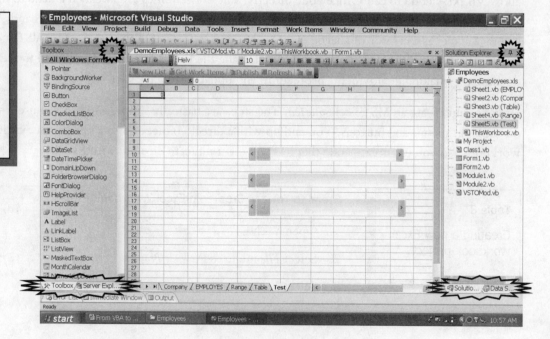

2.3   Connecting to Office Applications

In VBA, you could communicate with Excel directly because VBA was integrated into the application and the VB code was stored inside the document. And if you wanted to interact with another application, say Word, from inside Excel, you could reference the *Word Object Library* and then create an instance of the Word application:

```
Dim wdApp As New Word.Application
```

From there on, you were able to use the new object's *Documents.Open* method or apply the *GetObject()* function. So, why would you need VSTO, you may wonder. Well, VSTO shares its environment with .NET – and this combination makes for a much richer and more sophisticated tool (more integration, better data connections, higher speed, improved security, better deployment, and more languages from which to choose). Just keep reading!

A similar story holds for the difference between *VB 6.0* and *Visual Studio .NET*: *VB* already has the capacity to create instances of Excel and other Office application in order to use their properties, methods, and functions. So the question is again: Why would you go for VSTO? Because VSTO can interact directly with Office Applications! Office 2003+ comes with *PIAs* (*Primary Interop Assemblies*) that allow VB.NET code to call Office code directly. These assemblies are tweaked a little to make them perform better and more efficiently. The advantages can go either way: On the one hand, VSTO can leverage Excel as a creator of charts, pivot tables, and so forth. On the other hand, VSTO can create much more powerful assemblies – not located inside the Excel document but linked to the Excel document – making deployment, protection, and updating much easier.

How do you create an MS Excel *Solution*? The steps are basically simple and just require some clicking on the right menus and buttons. You end up with a direct connection to a new or an existing Excel workbook, so you can create code that lets you communicate directly with Excel.

Table 8 Creating a new Excel workbook project	Steps to Take – Create an Excel Workbook Project
	1. Open VS.NET.
	2. Select *File* menu → *New* → *Project*.
	3. Select *Visual Basic Projects*.
	4. Select the category *Office*.
	5. Select *Excel Workbook* → set its name.
	6. The *Project Wizard* kicks in and lets you choose whether to create a new Workbook or to attach the new assembly to an existing Workbook.

Figure 5

Project
template
options

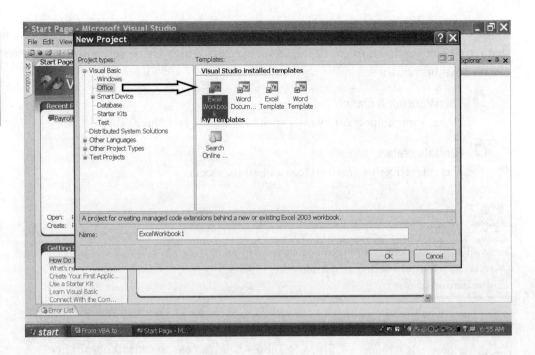

Now the Solution (or its project) contains at least two source files:

> ➤ *AssemblyInfo.vb*, which stores assembly-level metadata

> ➤ *ThisWorkbook.vb*, containing a single class called *ThisWorkbook*

How is the connection between document (*.xls*) and code (*.dll*) established? The connection is located in a property setting for the document that uses the assembly's name and location. You can find this information when you run the project and check Excel's properties: *File → Properties → Custom*.

Figure 6

Opening
document
property
settings

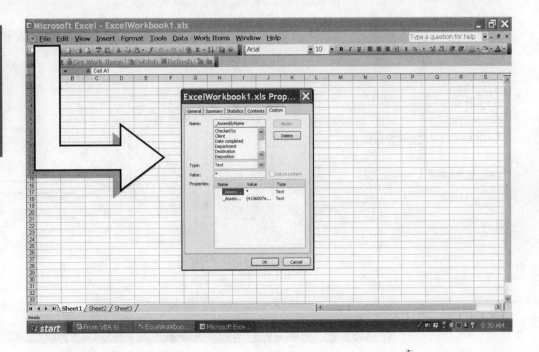

What is it that VSTO has created for you in the background? One of the ways to view the new Objects that have been created is to check the *ClassDiagram1.cd* file. There you will see that two important classes have been made:

ThisWorkbook class

Holds some important events, such as *Startup*() and *Shutdown*()

Globals class

Has references to *ThisWorkbook* and all its sheets

 Note:

You will need this *Globals* class when you want to refer to *ThisWorkbook* from "outside" the *ThisWorkbook.vb* file.

Table 9

Directions for adding Class Diagrams to Solutions Explorer

Steps to Take – Gain access to *ClassDiagram1.cd*

1. Right-click *ThisWorkBook* (or a Sheet) in the *Solution Explorer*.

2. Choose *Class Diagram*.

3. Expand both Objects with ⊕.
   You can also right-click any Object and then Choose *Class Details*.

4. Each new *Class Diagram* you have opened will be added to the *Solution Explorer*.

Figure 7

Class Diagrams added to Solutions Explorer

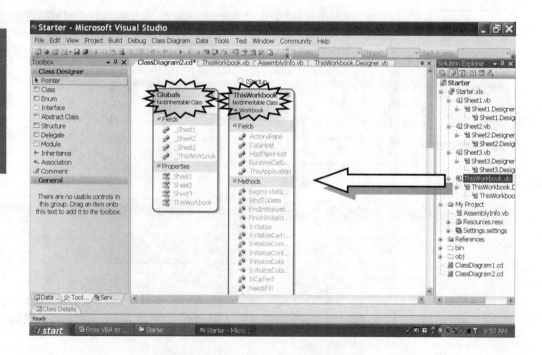

What else does VSTO do behind the scenes? It creates a tremendous amount of code that you don't see, and probably don't want to see (see 2.4). In order to make this "hidden" code visible, you may have to click one of the top buttons in the *Solution Explorer* – the *Show All Files* button. After doing so, you will see the following code when double-clicking on *ThisWorkbook.Designer.vb*:

Figure 8

Show all button makes hidden code visible

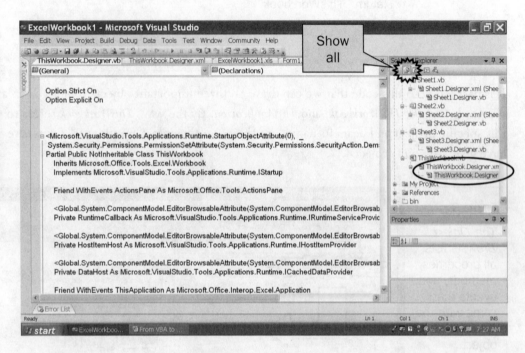

Notice how this code actually creates the *ThisWorkbook* and *Globals* classes. An ellipsis (…) indicates where I have shortened the code to make it look more palatable:

 Note:

Certain parts of the code may be marked as incorrect until you run the code with the ▶ button on the top toolbar (or use the *Debug* menu → *Start Debugging*).

```
Partial Public NotInheritable Class ThisWorkbook
    Inherits Microsoft.Office.Tools.Excel.Workbook
    Friend WithEvents ThisApplication As Microsoft.Office.Interop.Excel.Application
    …
    Dim hostObject As Object = Nothing
        Me.ThisApplication = CType(hostObject,Microsoft.Office.Interop.Excel.Application)
        Globals.ThisWorkbook = Me
        …
        Me.BeginInitialization
        …
    Public Overrides Sub OnShutdown()
        Implements Microsoft.VisualStudio….OnShutdown
        MyBase.OnShutdown
    End Sub
```

```
Partial Friend NotInheritable Class Globals
    Private Shared _ThisWorkbook As ThisWorkbook
    Friend Shared Property ThisWorkbook() As ThisWorkbook
      Get
        Return _ThisWorkbook
      End Get
      …
    End Property
```

It is partly due to this code that we can draw on three important objects to help us create all the code we need: *Globals*, *ThisWorkbook*, and *ThisApplication*. By the way, *ThisWorkbook* refers to the workbook in this specific project and bears its name – in this case, the name "Employees" (or whatever name you have given to your project).

Figure 9

The *Object Browser* lists all properties, methods, and events that come with the *ThisWorkBook* object.

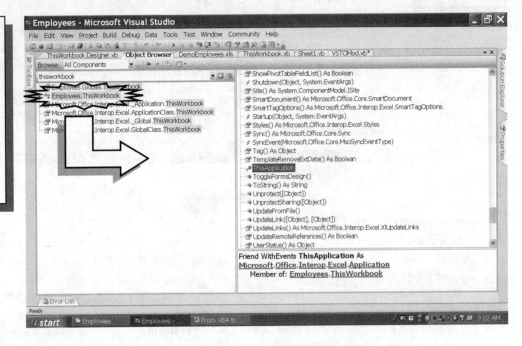

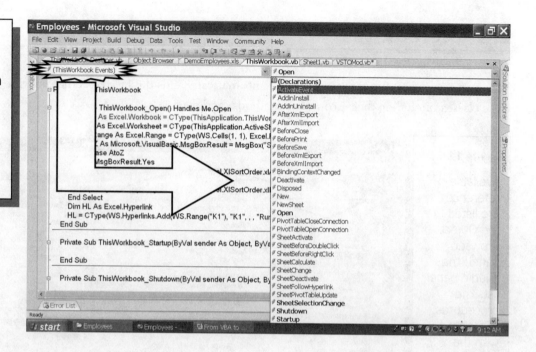

Figure 10

The events that come with *ThisWorkbook* also show up when you open the dropdown box for events.

Two of these Workbook events will have already been implemented when you open the window for *ThisWorkbook.vb*: Notice the *ThisWorkbook_Startup*() and *ThisWorkbook_Shutdown*() events.

```
Public Class ThisWorkbook
    Private Sub ThisWorkbook_Startup(ByVal sender As Object, ByVal e As _
        System.EventArgs) Handles Me.Startup
    End Sub
    Private Sub ThisWorkbook_Shutdown(ByVal sender As Object, ByVal e As _
        System.EventArgs) Handles Me.Shutdown
    End Sub
End Class
```

Whatever code you write in *ThisWorkbook_Startup* event will kick in when you load the Excel file. By the way, a *Startup* event kicks in before an *Open* event.

```
    Private Sub ThisWorkbook_Startup(ByVal sender As Object, ByVal e As _
        System.EventArgs) Handles Me.Startup
        MsgBox("This is my first VSTO project")
    End Sub
```

So what we have to work with now is a set of important objects that allow us to access elements such as *Selection* on any Excel spreadsheet in *ThisWorkbook*.

These are all legal statements inside *ThisWorkbook*:

➤ var = Application.Selection

➤ var = Me.Application.Selection

➤ var = ThisApplication.Selection

➤ var = Me.ThisApplication.Selection

2.4   References

When you create an Excel project, VSTO automatically adds the *References* that provide you with some basic classes, including their properties methods, and events:

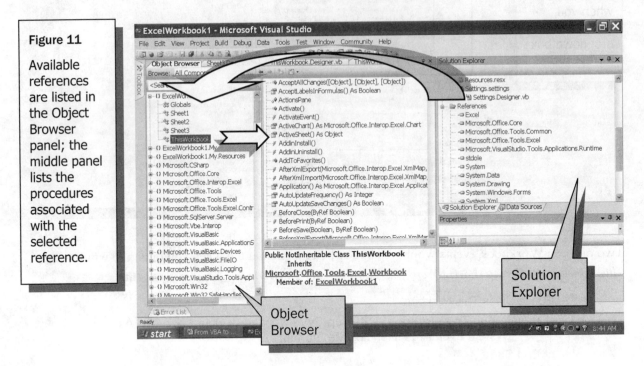

Figure 11

Available references are listed in the Object Browser panel; the middle panel lists the procedures associated with the selected reference.

The *Solution Explorer* has a section called *References*.

➢ When you double-click on one of those *References*, the *Object Browser* launches and lists all the available *References*.

➢ When you double-click one of those, the middle panel displays all the procedures that come with that specific reference.

The *References* listed in the *Solution Explorer* were automatically added, but you can also add your own references manually: Select *Project → Add Reference*.

Thanks to all this work done in the background, we can start building some simple code like the following:

Code Example 1: Regulating Application Settings

```
Public Class ThisWorkbook

    Private Sub ThisWorkbook_Startup(ByVal sender As Object, ByVal e As _
        System.EventArgs) Handles Me.Startup
      Dim bStat, bForm, bGrid As Boolean, sAddr As String
      If MsgBox("Statusbar?", MsgBoxStyle.YesNo) = MsgBoxResult.Yes Then bStat = True
      ThisApplication.DisplayStatusBar = bStat
      If MsgBox("Formulabar?", MsgBoxStyle.YesNo) = _
          MsgBoxResult.Yes Then bForm = True
      Application.DisplayFormulaBar = bForm
      If MsgBox("Gridlines?", MsgBoxStyle.YesNo) = MsgBoxResult.Yes Then bGrid = True
      ThisApplication.ActiveWindow.DisplayGridlines = bGrid
      ThisApplication.ActiveWindow.Zoom = InputBox("Set Zoom (50-400)", , "150")
      sAddr = InputBox("Which cell?", , "D5")
      ThisApplication.Goto(ThisApplication.Range(sAddr))
      ThisApplication.SendKeys("^{UP}")
    End Sub

    Private Sub ThisWorkbook_Shutdown(ByVal sender As Object, ByVal e As _
        System.EventArgs) Handles Me.Shutdown
      ThisApplication.DisplayStatusBar = True
      Application.DisplayFormulaBar = True
      ThisApplication.ActiveWindow.DisplayGridlines = True
    End Sub

End Class
```

Of course, you can also add modules to your Workbook, the way you used to do in VBA: *Project → Add Module → Select Module*. Modules provide a fitting place for your public procedures (former macros, methods, functions). Even if you create several modules (for grouping purposes and code maintenance), they will all be added to the same *.dll* file in time.

However, I have an important point to make: In these added modules, you cannot directly reference the object *ThisWorkbook* the way that you could in *ThisWorkbook.vb*. However, you can declare a variable in your modules that points to the *ThisWorkbook* class by using the *Globals* class, as mentioned earlier. It is probably wise to do so before typing any procedures. The code may look strange to you at first glance, but we will explain more about it soon.

```
Dim thisWB as Excel.Workbook = CType(Globals.ThisWorkbook, Excel.Workbook)
Dim S1 As Excel.Worksheet = CType(Globals.Sheet1, Excel.Worksheet)
```

Once you have tested a project – or rather a *Solution*, which is a container for one or more projects – you would normally close and save it. How do you open it again? In other words, on which file do you double-click? You will discover that the *Solution* contains quite a large number of files.

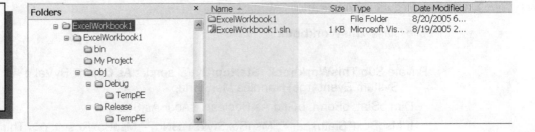

Figure 12

Solution folder's two elements

The *Solution* folder holds two elements at this stage:

🪟 **Another folder**
(usually, but not always)

🪟 **A .sln file**
(for your *Solution*)

The second folder holds three subfolders:

🐧 **Subfolder *bin***
Includes an *.xls* and a *.dll* file

🐧 **Subfolder *My Project***
Has all the files you see in the *Solution Explorer*

🐧 **Subfolder *obj***
Stores a *Debug* section (for the testing stage) and a *Release* section (once you are done with testing)

So which one of these files do you open if you want to work on your *Solution* again? You can double-click on the Project file (with a *.vbproj* extension) or – this is usually a better choice – you can double-click the *Solution* file (which has a *.sln* extension). Keep in mind, a *Solution* can contain more than one *Project*.

Table 10

Directions for opening a Solution

Steps to Take – Open an existing *Solution*
From VSTO:
1. *File → Open Project →* Double-click the *.sln* file.
2. OR: *File → Recent Projects →* select yours.
From the folder:
3. Double-click your Solution folder.
4. THEN: Double-click the .sln file.

2.5   What About Your Macros?

In VBA, you could run any subroutine as a macro – as long as the *Sub* didn't have any arguments. Remember, though, that VBA was stored in the *.xls* file as part of the Excel application, whereas VB.NET code is separate from the Excel file. So what does this mean when you migrate to VSTO?

The simplest solution is just to keep your macros in VBA (until Microsoft discontinues VBA) and to call these macros from your VSTO code. There are at least two ways of doing so:

➤ Use *ThisApplication.Run()* in a suitable event that comes with ThisWorkbook.

➤ Use *ThisApplication.OnKey()*, which allows you also to assign a shortcut key.
You would use this method in an event such as *ThisWorkbook_Open*, so the shortcut would be valid in the entire Workbook.

But if you decide to migrate your macrocode from VBA to VSTO, not only will you have to adjust the code (see the following chapters), but you will also need to decide how to call this subroutine. VBA macros used to reside inside the Excel file, which allowed them to be called from within Excel by using shortcut keys. VSTO modules, however, do not reside inside Excel but in a *.dll* assembly, so there is no direct calling option from inside Excel.

Say that you have transferred a former macro like the next one to *Module1*. What are your options in VSTO?

```
Module Module1

    Sub myFormerMacro()
        MsgBox("Running my former macro")
    End Sub

End Module
```

Here are a few of your calling options in VSTO:

1. Create a button on one (or a few) of your spreadsheets by dragging the button icon from the VSTO *Toolbox* to the spreadsheet (*.xls*). In the button's *Click* event, you could call the (former macro) procedure by just typing its name.

```
Public Class Sheet1

    Private Sub Button1_Click(...) Handles Button1.Click
        myFormerMacro()
    End Sub

End Class
```

2. Create a hyperlink in one of the cells of your spreadsheet and use the sheet's *FollowHyperlink* event. You can create the hyperlink by hand (Excel: *Insert → Hyperlink → Place in This Document →* etc.) or by code (in *ThisWorkbook_Open*), as I did in the following code:

Code Example 2: Creating Hyperlinks to Subroutines

```
Public Class ThisWorkbook

    Private Sub ThisWorkbook_Open() Handles Me.Open
        Dim WS As Excel.Worksheet = CType(ThisApplication.Sheets(1), Excel.Worksheet)
        WS.Activate()
        Dim HL As Excel.Hyperlink
        HL = CType(WS.Hyperlinks.Add (WS.Range("A1"), "", , , "Run Macro"), Excel.Hyperlink)
    End Sub

End Class
```

```
Public Class Sheet1

    Private Sub Sheet1_FollowHyperlink(ByVal Target As _
        Microsoft.Office.Interop.Excel.Hyperlink) Handles Me.FollowHyperlink
        If Target.TextToDisplay = "Run Macro" Then
            myFormerMacro()
        End If
    End Sub

End Class
```

3. Create a button on your Excel toolbar by using code in *ThisWorkbook*'s *Startup*() or *Open*() event.

Since the code is rather elaborate, we will skip this option here.

4. Call the code whenever the user hits a certain type of cell.

Code Example 3: Calling Subroutines from Certain Cell Types

```
Public Class Sheet1

    Private Sub Sheet1_SelectionChange(ByVal Target As _
        Microsoft.Office.Interop.Excel.Range) Handles Me.SelectionChange
        If IsDate(Target.Value) = True Then myFormerMacro()
    End Sub

End Class
```

5. Check for certain shortcut keys (such as *Ctr+Shift*) in an event closest to your needs – for instance, the event *SheetSelectionChange* (unfortunately, there is no *KeyPress* event for Workbooks yet).

Code Example 4: Calling Subroutines with Shortcut Keys

```
Public Class ThisWorkbook

    Private Sub ThisWorkbook_SheetSelectionChange(ByVal Sh As Object, _
        ByVal Target As Microsoft.Office.Interop.Excel.Range) _
        Handles Me.SheetSelectionChange
        Dim KS As New Microsoft.VisualBasic.Devices.Keyboard
        If KS.ShiftKeyDown And KS.CtrlKeyDown Then
            myFormerMacro()
        End If
    End Sub

End Class
```

6. And then there is the new *ActionsPane* that Office 2003 offers us. This pane is a perfect candidate for macro buttons and the like. However, it requires some fancy code, so we will postpone this issue until later (see 7.4).

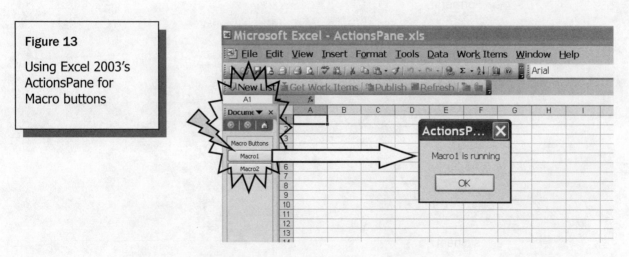

Figure 13

Using Excel 2003's ActionsPane for Macro buttons

Keep in mind that your former macros cannot directly reference such handy range objects as *ActiveCell* and *Selection* – because they are no longer global outside *ThisWorkbook*. In other words, you need to reference the *Globals* class or you must use variables for these *Range* objects when calling them from modules outside *ThisWorkbook* – regardless of whether they are regular modules, form modules (see 7), or class modules (see 11). In addition, you must specify which property you want to use, since VSTO has no default properties anymore.

Table 11			
Comparison of variables declaration in VBA vs. VSTO – note illegal definition using Selection	**Declare var in VBA**		Dim var As Range
	VBA		Set var = Selection
	Declare var in VSTO		Dim var As Excel.Range
	VSTO	**Illegal**	var = Selection
		Inside ThisWorkbook	var = Application.Selection.Value2
			var = ThisApplication.Selection.Value2
			var = Me.Application.Selection.Value2
			var = Me.ThisApplication.Selection.Value2
		Outside ThisWorkbook	var = Globals.ThisWorkbook.Application.Selection
			Dim **thisWB** As Excel.Workbook = _ CType(Globals.ThisWorkbook, Excel.Workbook)
			var = **thisWB**.Application.Selection.Value2

2.6   Case Study: A Rosetta Stone

In its left panel, each *Case Study* section shows which VBA code could have been used, and in its right panel, what would be a good alternative in VSTO (through VB.NET code). Thanks to this *Rosetta stone*, you will notice quite a few differences. At first sight, the new version may seem much more involved and long-winded to you, but you will probably also detect some huge advantages. Use any of the upcoming Rosetta stones as an aid in migrating your own VBA code to VSTO.

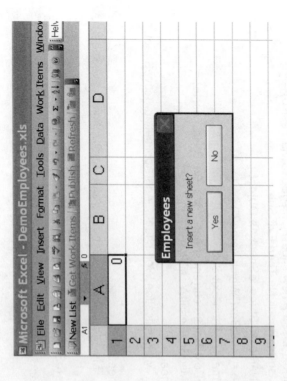

Figure 14

Screen that displays when code to insert a new sheet runs

The following code runs whenever users activate *Sheet2* in *ThisWorkbook*.

It will ask a few questions, and, depending on the user's answer, insert a new sheet with a specific name and at a specific position.

You could also change the code into a regular subroutine inside a *Module*, but then you might want to use one of the options we mentioned earlier in order to run the code from a *.dll* file inside Excel (see 2.4).

VBA

Code Example 5: Adding Sheets on Request

'In Sheet2

```vba
Private Sub Worksheet_Activate()
    If MsgBox("Insert a new sheet?", vbYesNo) = vbNo Then Exit Sub

    Dim sName As String, oSheet As Worksheet
    sName = InputBox("Which name?")
    If sName = "" Then Exit Sub
    If MsgBox("Before current sheet?", vbYesNo) = vbYes Then
        Set oSheet = _
            Me.Application.Worksheets.Add(Application.ActiveSheet)
    Else
        Set oSheet = _
            Me.Application.Worksheets.Add(, Application.ActiveSheet)
    End If
    oSheet.Name = sName
End Sub
```

VSTO

Public Class Sheet2

```vb
Private Sub Sheet2_ActivateEvent() Handles Me.ActivateEvent
    If MsgBox("Insert a new sheet?", MsgBoxStyle.YesNo) = _
        MsgBoxResult.No Then Exit Sub

    Dim sName As String, oSheet As Object
    sName = InputBox("Which name?")
    If sName = "" Then Exit Sub
    If MsgBox("Before current sheet?", MsgBoxStyle.YesNo) = _
        MsgBoxResult.Yes Then
        oSheet = _
            Me.Application.Worksheets. Add(Application.ActiveSheet)
    Else
        oSheet = _
            Me.Application.Worksheets.Add(, Application.ActiveSheet)
    End If
    CType(oSheet, Excel.Worksheet).Name = sName
End Sub
```

End Class

Figure 15

Screen that displays when code to format rows with alternate striping runs

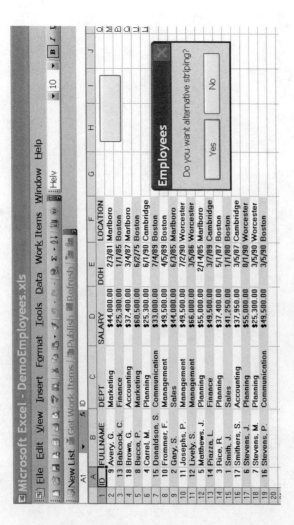

The following code runs whenever users activate *Sheet3*, which holds a database starting in cell *A1*. The users will be asked whether they want alternative striping in their database.

If their answer is yes, a dialog box will pop up with a choice of pattern colors. Be aware that this dialog box does not return a color but applies a color to the *ActiveCell*. So the code checks which color was applied and then applies this color to every other row in the *CurrentRegion*.

VBA

Code Example 6: Creating a Colored Striping Pattern in a Table

```
'In Sheet3

Private Sub Worksheet_Activate()

Dim myRegion As Range, iColor As Integer, i As Integer

Range("A1").Select
Set myRegion = ActiveCell.CurrentRegion
```

VSTO

```
Public Class Sheet3

    Private Sub Sheet3_ActivateEvent() Handles Me.ActivateEvent

        Dim WS As Excel.Worksheet = _
            CType(Me.Application.ActiveSheet, Excel.Worksheet)
        Dim AC As Excel.Range = CType(WS.Range("A1"), Excel.Range)
        AC.Select()
        Dim myRegion As Excel.Range = AC.CurrentRegion
```

From VBA to VSTO: Is Excel's New Engine for You?

VBA

```vb
If MsgBox("Do you want alternative striping?", vbYesNo) = _
    vbNo Then

    myRegion.Interior.ColorIndex = 0
Else
    Application.Dialogs(xlDialogPatterns).Show
    iColor = ActiveCell.Interior.ColorIndex
    myRegion.Interior.ColorIndex = 0
    For i = 1 To myRegion.Rows.Count Step 2

        myRegion.Rows(i).Interior.ColorIndex = iColor
    Next
End If
End Sub
```

VSTO

```vb
If MsgBox("Do you want alternative striping?", _
    MsgBoxStyle.YesNo) = MsgBoxResult.No Then

    myRegion.Interior.ColorIndex = 0
Else
    Application.Dialogs (Excel.XlBuiltInDialog.xlDialogPatterns).Show()
    Dim oColor As Object = AC.Interior.ColorIndex
    myRegion.Interior.ColorIndex = 0
    For i As Integer = 1 To myRegion.Rows.Count Step 2
        Dim myRow As Excel.Range = CType(myRegion.Rows(i), _
            Excel.Range)
        myRow.Interior.ColorIndex = oColor

    Next
End If
End Sub

End Class
```

3   Structure of the Language (VB.NET)

3.1   The Hierarchy of the Base Classes

VB.NET is much more object-oriented than VB was. What is an *Object*? An *Object* is an instance of a *Class*. Therefore, an *Object* first has to be <u>declared</u> to be a specific type of *Class*; it then has to be <u>created</u> as an instance of that particular *Class*.

	Declaring/Creating	Syntax
Table 12 There are several ways of declaring and creating *Objects*	Declaring	Dim Col As Collection
		Col.Add(...)
	Creating	Col = **New** Collection
		Col.Add(...)
	Declaring and Creating	Dim Collection As **New** Collection
		Col.Add(...)
	Declaring and Creating	Dim Col As Collection = **New** Collection
		Col.Add(...)

Let us take another example of this wide-ranging class approach. I am sure you remember that simple *Rnd()* function from VBA for those moments when you needed a random number. Well, VSTO has a *Random* class instead. Therefore, you have to create an instance of that class if you want to use one of its functions to return a specific random number. The class' *Next()* function, for instance, has a parameter that allows you to specify the range of integers you want to be returned; a setting of 10 returns integers between 0 and 9. The new code would be as follows:

```
Dim oRand As Random = New Random
Dim iRand as Integer = oRand.Next(10)
```

Because VB.NET is so thoroughly object-oriented, classes have a strictly "layered" hierarchical structure that often results in long addresses such as this one:

```
Me.Timer1 = New System.Windows.Forms.Timer(Me.components)
```

Why such long addresses? The answer is simple: VB.NET uses a hierarchy of base-classes and sub-classes in the background. This hierarchy is basically a relationship of base-class, sub-class, sub-sub-class, and so forth. So you have to drill the "address" down from "top" to "bottom." The concept behind this structure is *inheritance* – that is, reusing existing components (in base-classes, or parent-classes) by adding new parts or replacing older parts (in sub- or child-classes), so the lower class is said to "inherit" from the higher class (see 11.2 for more information on classes).

All objects in VB.NET, without exception, inherit from the base-class *System.Object* or from another class that inherits from that base class. If you want to call a different base-class, you must specify it by using its long hierarchical address – for instance: *System.Windows.Forms*. When creating an instance of *Form1* (see 7.1), you actually use *Form1* as a sub-class of the Form's base-class: *System.Windows.Forms*. The *Object Browser* can show you the structure of the inheritance tree as you "drill down" to the sub-classes.

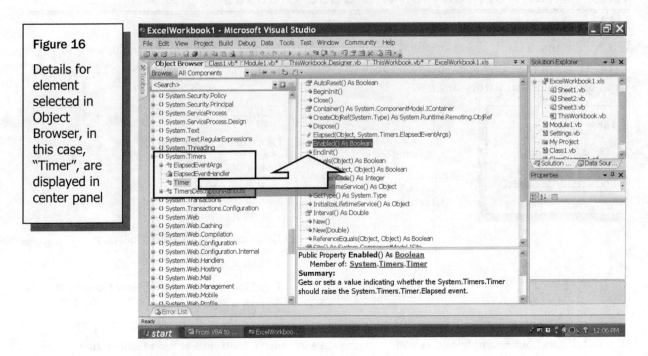

Figure 16

Details for element selected in Object Browser, in this case, "Timer", are displayed in center panel

The *Object Browser* is in the left panel (*View → Object Browser*).

➢ One of the base classes is *System.Timers*.

➢ One of its inherited members is: *System.Timers.Timer* (middle).

➢ One of that member's properties is: *Enabled*.

Because the *.NET Framework* provides huge numbers of classes in the system's class libraries, there is a strong need to group related classes together; this is done with *namespaces*. All classes are part of a namespace called *System*. The *System* namespace is very large, so it is subdivided into a number of subordinate namespaces, such as *System.Diagnostics*. Thanks to these subdivisions, the compiler is able to find what you are searching for – in this case, *System.Diagnostics.Debug.Write("...")*.

Figure 17

The *Class View* Window provides a listing of all classes used in your project plus all of their methods available to you.

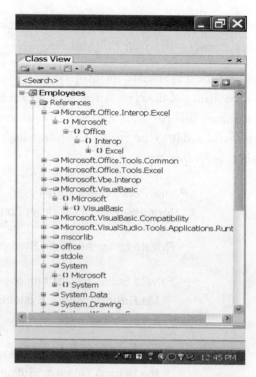

The *Class View* Window shows very clearly the hierarchical tree structure of base-classes and their sub-classes.

Most of these *References* were automatically added to the project. Others were done manually.

If you want to make a whole group of classes available at once, use the keyword *Imports* to make a certain *namespace* of related classes more easily accessible to the developer. This keyword offers you a smart way of avoiding a long address such as *System.Diagnostics.Debug.Write("...")*. Just call all related classes by their namespace name at the head of the code: *Imports System.Diagnostics*. From then on, you can just type the much shorter code: *Debug.Write("...")*. In this way, you can tell the compiler that you use functions and methods in that namespace so often that you want to be on a "first-name" basis with them. Had you only imported the *System* namespace, you would need to qualify much further: *Diagnostics.Debug.Write("...")*.

Table 13 System import options	Import	Syntax
		System.Diagnostics.Debug.Write("")
	Imports System	Diagnostics.Debug.Write("")
	Imports System.Diagnostics	Debug.Write("")

Namespaces have another benefit: They separate functions and methods that bear the same name. Thanks to namespaces, you can distinguish between them and thereby avoid conflicts.

Table 14 Differences between Imports, Inherits, and Implements keywords	Keyword	Description
	Imports	Imports the namespace of a specific library of related classes so your code can use a (sub-)class within that namespace with a shorter reference.
	Inherits	Makes a class gain all the behaviors of another class, so you don't have to implement them yourself.
	Implements	Allows you to create objects with more than one interface (not discussed in this book).

It is also possible to assign the namespace itself to a variable, which then acts as an alias: *Imports Excel = Microsoft.Office.Interop.Excel*.

To include a Form into the project, you actually create a new Class (say, *Form1*) and you then apply the functionality of the class *System.Windows.Forms.Form* by using the *Inherits* keyword. This functionality includes a title bar with buttons, a frame, and so on. Then you create a new instance of, say, the *Button* class and add it to the Form. The following code has been shortened to show the automatic results of your designing steps.

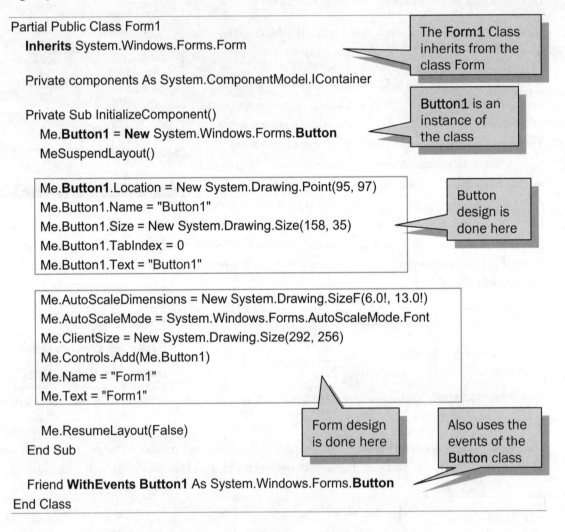

```
Partial Public Class Form1
    Inherits System.Windows.Forms.Form

    Private components As System.ComponentModel.IContainer

    Private Sub InitializeComponent()
        Me.Button1 = New System.Windows.Forms.Button
        MeSuspendLayout()

        Me.Button1.Location = New System.Drawing.Point(95, 97)
        Me.Button1.Name = "Button1"
        Me.Button1.Size = New System.Drawing.Size(158, 35)
        Me.Button1.TabIndex = 0
        Me.Button1.Text = "Button1"

        Me.AutoScaleDimensions = New System.Drawing.SizeF(6.0!, 13.0!)
        Me.AutoScaleMode = System.Windows.Forms.AutoScaleMode.Font
        Me.ClientSize = New System.Drawing.Size(292, 256)
        Me.Controls.Add(Me.Button1)
        Me.Name = "Form1"
        Me.Text = "Form1"

        Me.ResumeLayout(False)
    End Sub

    Friend WithEvents Button1 As System.Windows.Forms.Button
End Class
```

Callouts:
- The **Form1** Class inherits from the class Form
- **Button1** is an instance of the class
- Button design is done here
- Form design is done here
- Also uses the events of the **Button** class

The *References* that have been added to the project – either automatically or by your intervention – can be made visible in many different ways. There are two Windows in particular that show you all *References:* the *Solution Explorer* and the *Class View* Window.

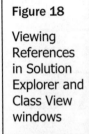

Figure 18

Viewing References in Solution Explorer and Class View windows

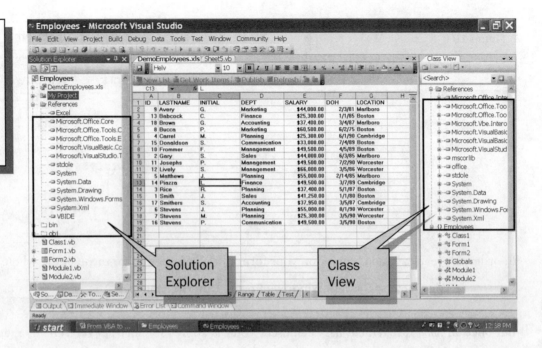

Table 15   Notice the correct order and location of keywords in the first example below.

Option Explicit On	Public Class Form1	Public Class Form1	Option Explicit On
Imports System.Math	Option Explicit On	Option Explicit On	Imports System.Math
Public **Class** Form1	Imports System.Math	Imports System.Math	Dim oAcc As Class1 Dim thisWB As …
Dim oAcc As Class1 Dim thisWB As …	Dim oAcc As Class1 Dim thisWB As …	Dim oAcc As Class1 Dim thisWB As …	Public Class Form1

Private Sub _
  Form1_Load(…) …
  …
End Sub
	Private Sub _
	  Form1_Load(…) …
	  …
	End Sub
		Private Sub _
		  Form1_Load(…) …
		  …
		End Sub
			Private Sub _
			  Form1_Load(…) …
			  …
			End Sub

End **Class**	End Class	End Class	End Class

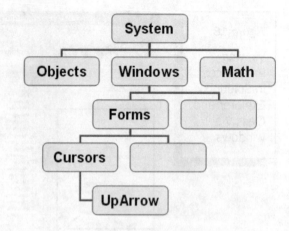

Figure 19

System hierarchy for Cursors

In order to create a "Hand" cursor on your form (*Me*), you need to go through the whole hierarchy:

Me.Cursor = **System.Windows.Forms.Cursors.Hand**

But once an *Imports* statement has been used, you can apply the short-cut referencing method:

Imports System.Windows.Forms

Public Class ...

    Sub ...
      Me.Cursor = **Cursors.Hand**
    End Sub

End Class

3.2   Core Objects

Now that you are capable of using some important *Objects*, you can manipulate Excel in a way very similar to what you used to do in VBA. Some names may have changed, many options have been expanded, and all of these are in the new syntax of VB.NET. Just try the properties and methods you have used in VBA, and find out what has changed and what has not.

In the next outline, I will only discuss the four core objects of Excel with some of their most important properties, methods, and events. These four core objects are:

> ➢ Excel.Application

> ➢ Excel.Workbook

> ➢ Excel.Worksheet

> ➢ Excel.Range

Sound familiar? Take advantage of these four classes! Not only do they contain powerful collections (such as *Workbooks*, *Sheets*, *Rows*), but also many great methods, functions, and events.

Be aware of some caveats, though. The first one: *Workbook*, *Worksheet*, and *Range* are part of the Excel namespace, so you need to qualify them more extensively (not *Range* but *Excel.Range*).

	VBA	VSTO
Table 16 Class qualification differences between VBA and VSTO	Dim AC As Range	Dim AC As **Excel**.Range
	Dim AW As WorkSheet	Dim AW As **Excel**.WorkSheet
	Dim WB As WorkBook	Dim WB As **Excel**.WorkBook

A second warning: Those very handy VBA shortcuts – *ActiveSheet*, *ActiveCell*, *Selection* – belong now to the *Application* object, so you need a much longer address to reference them.

	VBA	VSTO
Table 17 Reference differences between VBA and VSTO	ActiveSheet	**ThisWorkbook.Application**.ActiveSheet
	ActiveCell	**ThisWorkbook.Application**.ActiveCell
	Selection	**ThisWorkbook.Application**.Selection

ThisWorkbook, on the other hand, is a shortcut for the workbook associated with the project – which may not always be the <u>active</u> workbook!

One more reminder: *Application* properties such as *ActiveWorkbook*, *ActiveSheet*, *ActiveCell*, *Selection*, etc., return an *Object*! In other words, they do NOT return a *WorkBook* or *WorkSheet* or *Range* type. Therefore, you may need *CType()* conversions if your *Option Strict* is set to *On* (see 5.1.3). This is very crucial when you need one of their properties or methods; those can only be accessed after you cast the *Object* type into a *Range* type. Do you miss VBA already? Bear with me.

VBA:
```
Dim sAddr As String
sAddr = Selection.Address
```

VSTO:
```
Dim sAddr As String
sAddr = CType(Application.Selection, Excel.Range).Address
```

In other words, you have a choice to either declare a variable of the general *Object* type (and then use *CType()* later on to access its properties) or declare a variable of a more specific type by using *CType()* immediately (so you can later access its properties directly).

Either:
```
Dim SEL As Object = Application.Selection
Dim sAddr As String = CType(SEL, Excel.Range).Address
```

Or:
```
Dim SEL As Excel.Range = CType(Application.Selection, Excel.Range)
Dim sAddr As String = SEL.Address
```

And what do you think about this one?

| VBA: | ```Dim rSel As Range
Set rSel = Application.Inputbox("Select Range",, Selection.Address,,,,8)``` |
|------|---|
| VSTO: | ```Dim rSel As Excel.Range = CType(ThisWorkbook.Application.Inputbox _
    ("Select Range",, CType(ThisWorkbook.Application.Selection, _
    Excel.Range).Address,,,,8), Excel.Range)``` |

One last remark pertains to events. Many objects share similar events. Take for instance the *Change* event for *WorkBooks* and *Sheets*:

➤ As an event provided by the class *ThisWorkbook*, this *Change* event is called a *SheetChange* event, and is raised for any sheet currently open within Excel. This event handler passes an *Object* variable containing a reference to the sheet (*Sh*) plus a *Range* variable referring to the changed range (*Target*).

```
Private Sub ThisWorkbook_SheetChange(ByVal Sh As Object, ByVal Target As _
    Microsoft.Office.Interop.Excel.Range) Handles Me.SheetChange
```

➤ As an event provided by the *Worksheet* class, however, the event is just called a *Change* event (instead of *SheetChange*), so of course it does not pass a reference to the sheet – only to the range (*Target*).

```
Private Sub Sheet1_Change(ByVal Target As Microsoft.Office.Interop.Excel.Range) _
    Handles Me.Change
```

Table 18

Examples of properties, methods, and events in four different Classes

Some	Application	Excel.Workbook	Excel.Worksheet	Excel.Range
Properties	Workbooks ThisApplication ThisWorkbook WorksheetFunction ActiveCell / Active… / Selection ScreenUpdating DisplayAlerts	Sheets FullPath / Name / Path Password PrecisionAsDisplayed Styles	Rows Columns Outlines Comments	Rows Columns Address CurrentRegion Offset EntireRow EntireColumn
Methods	Calculate FileDialog MailSystem SendMail FindControl	Activate Save Close Protect	Protect PrintOut Calculate	Group Union / Intersect / Areas Find Sort Autofill

Some	Application	Excel.Workbook	Excel.Worksheet	Excel.Range
Events	SheetActivate SheetChange SheetFollowHyperlink WorkbookActivate	SheetActivate SheetChange SheetFollowHyperlink WorkbookActivate	Activate Change FollowHyperlink	

3.3   Host Controls

Host (or *View*) controls are controls that extend existing Excel objects. Why would you ever want to use these? Because they include events and special data-binding capabilities (see 10.4)! These additions give you much more leverage. You can just drag these controls from the *Excel Controls* section in the VSTO *Toolbox* and drop them onto the document. Then you can use their specific events and methods.

These are Excel's three *Host* Controls:

 NamedRange is an extension of the *Range* object.
If something changes in this range, the Control's *Change* event will notify you (otherwise, you would have to use the *SheetChange* event and then find out whether the change was in the range you were interested in).

 **Caution!**

Be aware that if you change a value through the *Change* event, you will go into an endless loop of *Change* events.

Table 19 Directions for inserting a Named Range

Steps to Take – Inserting a NamedRange

1. Go to the Excel spreadsheet in the VSTO Editor.

2. Expand in the *Toolbox* the Section *Excel Controls*.

3. Drag the *NamedRange* control (a class) onto *Sheet1,* which has data on it, including a series of salaries.

4. Assign a reference (e.g., *B2:B10*, filled here with salaries).

5. Go to *Sheet1.vb* and use events of *NamedRange1* (an object).

 ListObject is a range that extends multiple columns and rows.
It also supports sorting on any column and is the only *Host* control that supports complex data binding by binding to more than one value (see 3.3). We will get back to it in 10.4.

 Chart is an extension of the Chart object.

In the example of a *NamedRange,* as created by the previous steps, you could implement the following code – which would undo changes to the *NamedRange* if the user did not know the password.

Code Example 7: Checking Changes in a Named Range with a Password

```
Public Class Sheet1

    Dim old As String

    Private Sub NamedRange1_SelectionChange(ByVal Target As _
        Microsoft.Office.Interop.Excel.Range) Handles NamedRange1.SelectionChange
        old = CType(Target.Value2, String)
    End Sub

    Private Sub NamedRange1_Change(ByVal Target As _
        Microsoft.Office.Interop.Excel.Range) Handles NamedRange1.Change
        If CType(Target.Value2, String) = old Then Exit Sub
        If InputBox("Password", , "secret") <> "secret" Then
            Application.Undo()
        End If
    End Sub

End Class
```

Thanks to *NamedRange* events such as *SelectionChange* and *Change*, we can exploit the information that was passed through the variable *Target*. It is a simple control that can save lots of programming steps.

3.4 Case Study: A Rosetta Stone

Figure 20

Screen that displays when code to check the user's password runs

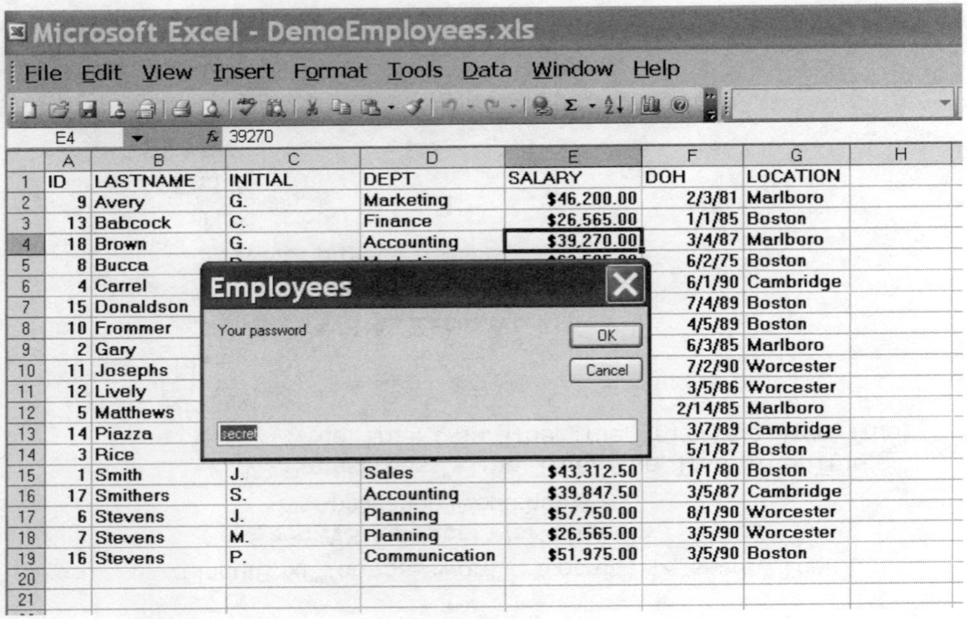

The following code checks the password when *ThisWorkbook* starts (the *Startup* event kicks in before the *Open* event).

If the password is correct, all Worksheets will be unprotected; otherwise they will all be protected.

Code Example 8: Protecting and Unprotecting Sheets with a Password

VBA Version	VSTO Version

VBA Version

```vba
'In WorkBook

Private Sub Workbook_Open()

Dim WS As Worksheet
If InputBox("Your password", , "secret") <> "secret" Then
    For Each WS In Worksheets

        WS.Protect "pass", True, True, True

    Next
Else
    For Each WS In Worksheets

        WS.Unprotect "pass"

    Next
End If
End Sub
```

VSTO Version

```vbnet
Public Class ThisWorkbook

Private Sub ThisWorkbook_Startup(ByVal sender As Object, _
    ByVal e As System.EventArgs) Handles Me.Startup

If InputBox("Your password", , "secret") <> "secret" Then
    For Each WS As Excel.Worksheet In _
        ThisApplication.Worksheets
        WS.Protect("pass", True, True, True, True, _
            True, True, True, True, True, True)

    Next
Else
    For Each WS As Excel.Worksheet In _
        ThisApplication.Worksheets
        WS.Unprotect("pass")

    Next
End If
End Sub

End Class
```

4   Syntax Changes in VB.NET

Since we have already used some VB.NET code, you may be wondering why the code is structured the way it is – which can be quite different from what you were used to in VBA. Now it is time to investigate the differences between both languages in more detail.

What hasn't changed is the fact that *Objects* have:

> ➤ Properties (see 4.1)

> ➤ Methods and Functions (see 4.2)

> ➤ Events (see 0)

But certain things about these components did change in the process. We will just address the main issues that you need to know in order to make the transition from VBA to VSTO.

4.1   Properties

Unlike VB, VB.NET does not acknowledge *default* properties. This is most likely a problem for those VBA programmers who have nurtured the habit of not typing default properties such as the property *Value* for objects like *Range* and *Cells*. Skipping or omitting former-default properties creates runtime errors in VB.NET. So you must eradicate this habit. That's good policy anyway, because it is helpful for debugging purposes to visually show which property was used. Besides, it avoids ambiguities in command lines like these: *Text1* = *"Hallo"* – where the question would be whether *Text1* is a variable or the name of a *TextBox* object.

Table 20 Differences in command line syntax between VBA and VSTO	VBA	VSTO
	TextBox1 = 10	TextBox1 = 10
	TextBox1.Text = 10	TextBox1.**Text** = 10
	ActiveCell = 10	ActiveCell = 10
	ActiveCell.Value = 10	ActiveCell.**Value** = 10
	ActiveCell.Value2 = 10	ActiveCell.**Value2** = 10

The only difference between the *Value* and the *Value2* property is that the *Value2* property doesn't use the *Currency* and *Date* data types. You can return values formatted with these data types as floating-point numbers by using the *Double* data type. And as to *Value*, you can specify the *ValueDataType* as a parameter. See more on data types in 5.1.

In this context, we should also specifically mention those properties that must be set to *enumeration constants*. Think of the many *xl...* constants in VBA, such as *xlAscending*, *xlCenter*, and so forth. Compared with VBA, VSTO makes two major changes to enumeration constants:

1. Enumeration settings are more long-winded in VB.NET. The reason for this is that these constants are no longer *global*, as they used to be in VBA. So you cannot call them directly, but must use the fully qualified enumeration name – that is, a long class-subclass address.

Table 21

Differences in enumeration syntax between VBA and VSTO

VBA	VSTO

ActiveCell.HorizontalAlignment = _
     xlCenter
	ActiveCell.HorizontalAlignment = _
	     Excel.XlHAlign.xlHAlignCenter

CurrentRegion.Sort(..., xlAscending)	CurrentRegion.Sort(..., **Excel.XlSortOrder**.xlAscending)
Application.Cursor = xlDefault	Application.Cursor = **Excel.XlMousePointer**.xlDefault

2. Another change is that constants' *names* cannot be replaced with constants' *numbers* anymore the way you could in VBA. If you did develop the habit of using numbers, you need to substitute numbers with names when migrating to VSTO.

Table 22

Differences in constant name syntax between VBA and VSTO

VBA	VSTO
Application.CutCopyMode = **1**	Application.CutCopyMode = **Excel.XlCutCopyMode.xlCopy**
CurrentRegion.Sort(..., **1**)	CurrentRegion.Sort(..., **Excel.XlSortOrder.xlAscending**)
cmdClick.MousePointer = **10**	btnClick.Cursor = **System.Windows.Forms.Cursors.UpArrow**

3. Finally, certain properties can only be set by calling a new instance of the proper class:

   ➢ Me.Font = **New Font**("Arial", 10, FontStyle.Bold)
   ➢ Me.Button1.Size = **New Size**(..., ...)
   ➢ Me.Button1.Location = **New Point**(..., ...)

Settings like these are very common in VB.NET. Just get used to it. In addition, some of these classes may carry much longer addresses: *Me.Button1.Size = New System.Drawing.Size* – unless there is a reference to this namespace at the head of the code: *Imports System.Drawing*.

One more comment. As we said before, VB.NET is much more consistent in its indexes than VB used to be: All indexes start at 0. However, where VSTO deals directly with Excel, it is tied to the indexes Excel uses – and many of those still begin at 1 (especially true in Collections such as *Rows*, *Columns*, *Worksheets*, etc.).

4.2 Methods and Functions

The difference in the way VBA treated methods (without parentheses) as opposed to functions (with parentheses) has become part of the past in VSTO. It doesn't matter anymore whether *MsgBox* is a function that returns something or a method that doesn't return anything. In both cases, you use parentheses; you are even required to use parentheses for methods when passing parameters in a method call.

So from now on, the method *MsgBox()* will look like this: *MsgBox ("Hallo", MsgBoxStyle.OK)*. The function *MsgBox()*, on the other hand, would look very similar: *var = MsgBox("Yes or No", MsgBoxStyle.YesNo)*. Even if a method does not require any arguments, the parentheses can still be there, although they are not mandatory – for instance, *Me.Close()*. By the way, it is good to know that *MsgBox(...)* can be replaced in VSTO with *MessageBox.Show(...)* – another indication of the fact that there is a class behind this object.

Table 23

Differences in method and function syntax between VBA and VSTO

MessageBoxes and InputBoxes		
	VBA	**VSTO**
MsgBox	MsgBox "…"	MsgBox("…")
		MessageBox.Show("…")
	If MsgBox("…", **vbYesNo**) = _ **vbYes** Then…	If MsgBox("…",, **MsgBoxStyle.YesNo**) = _ **MsgBoxResult.Yes** Then …
		If MessageBox.Show("…",, **MsgBoxStyle.YesNo**) = _ **MsgBoxResult.Yes** Then …
InputBox	sVar = InputBox("…")	sVar = InputBox("…")
	Set myRange = _ Application.InputBox("…",,,,,,, 8)	myRange = **CType**(Application.InputBox _ ("Select Range",,,,,,, 8), **Excel.Range**)

When creating your own methods and functions, be aware that VB.NET – unlike VB – passes arguments or parameters by value, so you do not need to insert the keyword *ByVal*. However, if you do want to change this behavior, you must include the keyword *ByRef*. By the way, in VB.NET you can also use the keyword *Return* instead of using the name of the function for a second time inside the function.

Here's another caveat. Functions or methods that can be called "directly" in VBA may require a longer address in VSTO. Take, for instance, the functions *Abs* and *Sqrt* (no longer *Sqr,* by the way); they now belong to the System's *Math* class. In order to call these functions, you need either a long or a short address; however, in the latter case, you need an *Imports* statement at the head of the code:

Table 24 — Differences in calling functions between VBA and VSTO	VBA	VSTO
	var = Sqr(4)	var = **System.Math**.Sqrt(4)
		Imports System.Math var = Sqrt(4)

You may also need to get used to the fact that many methods in VB.NET are "overloaded." *Overloading* means that a method can have several parameter lists (see also 11.2). A different parameter list means different data types in the list. The following would be an example of four overloaded methods:

- ➢ myMethod(X As Integer, Y As Integer)
- ➢ myMethod(X As Integer, Y As **Double**)
- ➢ myMethod(X As **Double**, Y As Integer)
- ➢ myMethod(X As **Double**, Y As **Double**)

Table 25

Differences in method and function syntax between VBA and VSTO

Overview of Differences in Methods and Functions	
VBA	**VSTO**
ActiveCell.Delete **xlUp**	Application.ActiveCell.Delete(**Excel.XlInsertShiftDirection.xlShiftDown**)
ActiveCell.Copy	**Application**.ActiveCell.Copy()
ActiveCell.PasteSpecial **xlPasteValues**	**Application**.ActiveCell.PasteSpecial(**Excel.XlPasteType.xlPasteValues**)

Function CubeRoot(num As Double) _
    As Double
    CubeRoot = num ^ (1/3)
 	
End Function
	Function CubeRoot(num As Double) As Double
	
	    CubeRoot = num ^ (1/3)
	    'OR: **Return** num ^ (1/3)
	End Function

Sub Expand(str As String)
    str = str & str
End Sub
	Sub Expand(**ByRef** str As String)
	    str = str & str
	End Sub

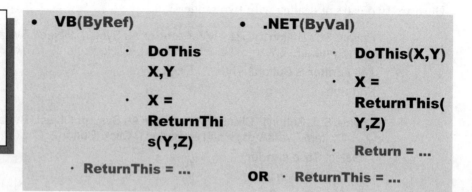

Figure 21

Differences in defaults (ByRef vs. ByVal), in use of parentheses, and in optional use of the *Return* keyword

Default: ➤ *ByVal* is the default in VB.NET.

Parentheses: ➤ Parentheses are also used for methods in VB.NET.

Return: ➤ You can use the *Return* keyword in VB.NET instead of the name of the function.

4.3   Events

When working with *UserForms*, *Workbooks*, or *Worksheets* in VB, you often must have relied on the power of event handlers such as *Button_Click*, *WorkBook_Open*, *Worksheet_SelectionChange*, etc. It probably won't surprise you that VB.NET has similar events (and many more), but their starting lines differ somewhat. Take the following line:

```
Private Sub Button1_Click(ByVal sender As System.Object, ByVal e As _
    System.EventArgs) Handles Button1_Click
```

The beginning of the line looks familiar, but the end is unusual. It features the keyword *Handles*. Why specify the same button again at the end? The answer is that you can use the same event handler for several buttons at the same time:

```
Private Sub Button1_Click(ByVal sender As System.Object, ByVal e As _
    System.EventArgs) Handles Button1_Click, Button2_Click
```

How would you know which button of those specified was actually clicked? The answer can be found through a parameter called *sender*, which is a *System.Object* outfitted with its own properties. We could say, for instance: *If sender Is Button1 Then … Else …* An alternative would be: *Select Case sender*. To get one of the object's properties, you may have to do a bit more: *sVar = CType(sender, Button).Text*.

Here are two ways of dealing with two senders:

```
Private Sub Button1_Click(ByVal sender As System.Object, ByVal e As _
    System.EventArgs) Handles Button1_Click, Button2_Click
    If sender Is Button1 Then … Else …
End Sub
```

```
Private Sub Button1_Click(ByVal sender As System.Object, ByVal e As _
    System.EventArgs) Handles Button1_Click, Button2_Click
    Select Case sender
        Case Button1: …
        Case Button2: …
    End Select
End Sub
```

In addition to covering several objects with the same event handler, it is also possible to create several event handlers that all respond to the same event – say, a click on a button triggers two different event handlers (which would both be handled by the same *Button1_Click*). Whichever event handler appears first in code will execute before the next event handler kicks in. You may want to apply this technique if you have two separate procedures that need to be combined only at certain occasions.

So the keyword here is *Handles*. It allows us to write multiple event handlers for a single event – or, reversed, a single event handler for multiple events. This feature offers us some nice flexibility.

4.4 Case Study: A Rosetta Stone

In this case study, we will add three *HScrollbar* controls to a Worksheet. These controls probably remind you of the controls you used to add to older versions of Excel by means of the *Control Toolbox* toolbar (which was one of the toolbars at the top of your Excel application). Now these controls have been incorporated into the VSTO environment.

Figure 22

Adding *HScrollbar* controls to a Worksheet

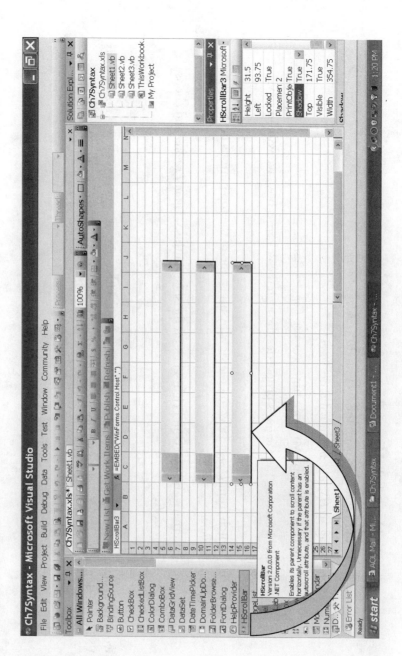

Table 26

Directions for adding *HScrollbar* controls to a Worksheet

Steps to Take – Adding Controls to a sheet

1. Double-click the correct sheet in the *Solution Explorer*.

2. In the *Toolbox*, expand the section *All Windows Forms*.

3. Drag an *HScrollbar* control onto *Sheet1*.

4. Repeat this step two more times (or use *Copy / Paste*).

Instead of setting the *Control's* properties through the *Properties* box, we will do so via code.

5. Switch from *Design* view to *Code* view by using one of the top buttons in the *Solution Explorer*.

6. Alternatively, you could right-click on the sheet in the *Solution Explorer* and choose *View Code*.

Through these three *HScrollbar* controls, we will regulate the cells' interior color. All of this is done with code, of course. You will notice quite a few differences. At first sight, the new VSTO version may seem much more involved and long-winded to you, but you will probably also detect some huge advantages over VBA.

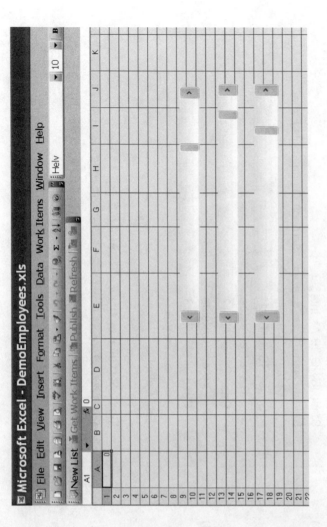

Figure 23

Adding *HScrollbar* controls to a Worksheet

The following code sets the maximum property of *HScrollbars* from 3 to 255 during launch time.

Each scrollbar regulates one of the three color components: red, green, and blue – running from 0 to 255. Here we use the function *RGB()* for the three color components.

From now on, scrolling one of the scrollbars will change colors in all cells of this worksheet: the color of the interior, the color of the borders, as well as the color of the font.

If you consider this a useless code, I don't blame you, but it may be a good starter to get used to VSTO. This *Rosetta* stone will show you where the two languages differ.

VBA Version	VSTO Version

Code Example 9: Regulating Background Colors with Scrollbars

VBA Version:

```vba
'In Sheet1
Dim iR, iG, iB As Long
Private Sub Worksheet_Activate()

    Me.ScrollBar1.Max = 255
    Me.ScrollBar2.Max = 255
    Me.ScrollBar3.Max = 255

End Sub
Private Sub ScrollBar1_Scroll()
    iR = Me.ScrollBar1.Value
    Me.Cells().Interior.Color = RGB(iR, iG, iB)
    Me.Cells().Borders.Color = RGB(255 - iR, 255 - iG, 255 - iB)
    Me.Cells().Font.Color = RGB(255 - iR, 255 - iG, 255 - iB)

End Sub
Private Sub ScrollBar2_Scroll()
    iG = Me.ScrollBar2.Value
    Me.Cells().Interior.Color = RGB(iR, iG, iB)
    Me.Cells().Borders.Color = RGB(255 - iR, 255 - iG, 255 - iB)
    Me.Cells().Font.Color = RGB(255 - iR, 255 - iG, 255 - iB)

End Sub
Private Sub ScrollBar3_Scroll()
    iB = Me.ScrollBar3.Value
    Me.Cells().Interior.Color = RGB(iR, iG, iB)
    Me.Cells().Borders.Color = RGB(255 - iR, 255 - iG, 255 - iB)
    Me.Cells().Font.Color = RGB(255 - iR, 255 - iG, 255 - iB)

End Sub
```

VSTO Version:

```vbnet
Public Class Sheet1

    Private Sub Sheet1_Startup(ByVal sender As Object, ByVal e As _
        System.EventArgs) Handles Me.Startup

        Me.HScrollBar1.Maximum = 255
        Me.HScrollBar2.Maximum = 255
        Me.HScrollBar3.Maximum = 255

    End Sub
    Private Sub HScrollBar1_Scroll(ByVal sender As System.Object, _
        ByVal e As System.Windows.Forms.ScrollEventArgs) Handles _
        HScrollBar1.Scroll, HScrollBar2.Scroll, HScrollBar3.Scroll

        Static iR, iG, iB As Integer
        Select Case CType(sender, Microsoft.Office.Tools.Excel. _
            Controls.HScrollBar).Name

            Case "HScrollBar1"
                iR = e.NewValue
            Case "HScrollBar2"
                iG = e.NewValue
            Case "HScrollBar3"
                iB = e.NewValue

        End Select

        Me.Cells().Interior.Color = RGB(iR, iG, iB)
        Me.Cells().Borders.Color = RGB(255 - iR, 255 - iG, 255 - iB)
        Me.Cells().Font.Color = RGB(255 - iR, 255 - iG, 255 - iB)

    End Sub
End Class
```

5   Changes in Data Types and Scope

5.1   Data Types

In VB.NET, all data types – *Value* types as well as *Reference* types – are defined in CTS: the *Common Types System*. One of these types, the *Object* type (see page 51), is in *System.Object*. CTS is also the system where all *Value* types are defined – *Booleans*, for instance, are in *System.Boolean*.

So, the message here is: *Data Types* have become *Objects* in VB.NET; that is, instances of *Classes!* Because *Data Types* are rooted in a certain class, they have their own "intelligence," so the class tells them how to "behave." In other words, they have properties, methods, and functions. An *Integer*, being an instance of the *Integer* class, knows the minimum and maximum value it can store (*MinValue*, *MaxValue*); it knows how to convert itself to a string (*ToString()*), and so on. Because *Data Types* are *Objects*, their *Classes* have some interesting methods that you may want to know about.

Table 27	System.	Example
Differences in *System.Objects, System.Data, System.Integer*, etc. syntax between VB and VB.NET	.Equals()	If var1.**Equals**(var2) Then …
	.ToString()	myDate.**ToString**("m/d/yyyy")
		Now().**ToString**("dddd m/d/yy")
		myString = mySingle.**ToString**("$ #,###.00")
	.GetType()	MsgBox("Type: " & myDouble.**GetType**()
	.MaxValue	MsgBox("Max: " & Long.**MaxValue**.ToString("#,###"))

Let us discuss these *Data Types* in more detail, especially as to the changes VB.NET has enforced. First, I would like you to look at this overview of the differences between *Value* type and *Reference* type:

Table 28	Value Type	Reference Type
Differences between *Value* type and *Reference* type	Used for a single piece of data	Holds the address of a location in memory (on the "heap") where many pieces of data may be stored
	Created on the "stack" (static)	Created on the "heap" (dynamic)
	–	Garbage Collection (see 11.3)
	–	Use the *New* keyword for creation
	If not created: "" or *0*	If not created: *Nothing*
	Equality check operator: =	Equality check operator: *Is*

Note:

Strings and *Arrays* are the odd balls here. Although they are of the *Reference* Type, they do not necessarily take the *New* keyword, plus their equality is tested with the equal-sign operator. However, *Arrays* can, and sometimes have to be, created with the *New* keyword (see 6.1).

5.1.1   Value Types

Value types are used for a single piece of data, which is stored in an area called the "stack" – a fixed amount of computer memory. With VB.NET, the most important change in *Value* types is their span:

- *Integers* range from four to eight bytes. If you wanted to loop through all 65536 rows in Excel, you had to use a variable of the *Long* type in VBA; but in VB.NET, you can use an *Integer* type.

- *Currency* (with eight bytes) has been replaced with the more capable *Decimal* (with 12 bytes). This is good news for those working with large numbers that should not be rounded internally, as *Single* and *Double* do.

- The huge size used by VBA *Variants* (16 bytes) has been abandoned in VB.NET to make place for the *Object* type. When you do not know a value's type at design time, make it of the *Object* type in VB.NET. This is called *Late-Binding*.

How do you declare types? The same way that you did in VBA, but with some nice improvements:

- You do not have to repeat the same type on the same line. These three variables are all of the *Double* type:

  Dim dOne, dTwo, dThree As **Double**

- Declaring and initializing (or even creating) a variable can be done at the same time:

  Dim dOne **As Double** *= 0.075*

- Even fancier combinations are possible since VS 2005:

  For i **As Integer** *= 10 To 20*

  For dim1 **As Long** *= 0 To arr.GetLength(0)-1*

Table 29

Overview of VBA type, VB.NET type, and underlying CTS type

VBA type	VB.NET type	Underlying CTS type
Boolean (2)	Boolean (4)	System.Boolean
Integer (2)	**Short** (4)	System.Int16
	Integer (4)	System.Int32
Long (**4**)	Long (**8**)	System.Int64
Single (4)	Single (4)	System.Single
Double (8)	Double (8)	System.Double
Currency (8)	**Decimal** (12)	System.Decimal

5.1.2   Reference Types

Unlike *Value* types, which are used for a single piece of data, *Reference* types contain the address (four bytes) of a dynamic block of memory (on the "heap") that changes its size depending on the application's requirements.

The following elements are of the *Reference* type: *Object*, *String*, *Array* (see 6.1), *Class* (see 11.1), *Interface*, and *Delegate*. As with *Value* types, you can combine the declaration and creation into one statement – in VS 2005+, you can do this even more comprehensively than you ever might have dreamed.

Table 30 *Reference* type elements	Reference Elements	
	Dim oNew As Object	
	Dim oClass As New myClass()	
	Dim oClass As myClass = New myClass()	
	For Each cell **As Excel.Range** In ....Range("A1:A10")	
	For Each WS **As Excel.Worksheet** In This Workbook.Worksheets	
	Catch ex **As Exception**	'See 8.1
	Imports myExcel = Microsoft.Office.Interop.Excel	'See 2.3
	Dim arr() **As Integer** = {1, 2, 3, 4, 5}	'See 6.1

As mentioned before, the *Value* type *Variant* has been replaced by the *Reference* type *Object*. Just as you used the *Variant* to store *Strings*, *Integers*, as well as classes in VBA, you can use *System.Object* to do the same in VSTO. However, this new *Object* type can do more than the *Variant* type could, because it is based on a class that exposes methods and functions such as *Finalize()*, *GetType()*, and *ToString()*.

Because the *Object* type can hold anything, it is always late-bound, so you may not be able to use properties and methods that are more specific. Each time you want to interact with the more specific properties and methods of an *Object* type variable, you must convert the general *Object* type to a more appropriate type by using the *CType()* function:

```
CType(obj, myClass).myMethod()
var = CType(obj, myClass).myProperty()
```

 Note:

There is also a rather similar conversion function called *DirectCast()*. However, *DirectCast()* requires an inheritance or implementation relationship between the data types of the two arguments (see 11.2). This means that one type must inherit from or implement the other – otherwise, you get an error.

What about objects that are not instances of the *Object* class, but of any other kind of class – say, an instance of the class called *myClass()*? We are definitely dealing here with a *Reference* type. In VBA, you would declare the object to be of a certain *Reference* type and then you would create it with the *Set* keyword. Be aware, though, that the *Set* keyword from VBA has been eliminated in VSTO. So when you split declaration from creation, you should not use the *Set* keyword when you actually create the object. All you need is this line: *oClass = New clsClass()*.

There is one more point to remember: If you declare a *Reference* type with the *New* keyword, VB.NET will create the instance of the class immediately – which is different from VBA where the creation did not take place until the *Set* keyword had been used. Notice also that the class itself requires parentheses:

Split or combined	Declaration
Split declaration and creation	Dim oClass As myClass() oClass = **New** myClass()
Combined declaration and creation	Dim oClass As **New** myClass()
	Dim oClass As myClass = **New** myClass()
	Dim **WithEvents** oClass As **New** myClass()

Table 31

Four equivalent ways of declaring and creating an *Object* as an instance of a *Class*

When declaration and creation are done at the same time, we speak of early-binding. The *New* keyword actually creates the object (unlike in VBA, where the code would keep checking whether the object had already been created) and it also determines its type. So when typing a *period* after the object's name, we get help in the form of a list of methods (which is called *IntelliSense*). Consequently, we can draw on *IntelliSense* when using the new variable, because all its properties and methods have been exposed already. If there is a problem in using one of these, the trouble will be discovered at compile-time (instead of later on, at run-time).

Finally, you should know that objects declared but not yet created are set to *Nothing*, so you can check them with the *IsNothing* function. This is different from VBA, since VBA objects would start as *Empty* and COM objects as *Nothing*. This inconsistency is eliminated in VSTO.

Table 32   Differences in declaration of objects between VBA and VSTO

VBA	VB.NET
Dim X As **Variant**	Dim X As **Object**
Dim X As **Integer**, Y As **Integer**	Dim X, Y As **Integer**
Dim X as Short X = 5	Dim X As Short **= 5**
Dim X As New myClass ⇨ *checks creation*	Dim X As New myClass() ⇨ *creates object*
Dim X As myClass **Set** X = New myClass	Dim X As myClass X = New myClass()

5.1.3   Conversion

More so than VBA, VSTO lets you control the way the compiler handles data types with *Option* statements:

Figure 24

*Tools →
Options →
Projects and
Solutions →
VB Defaults*

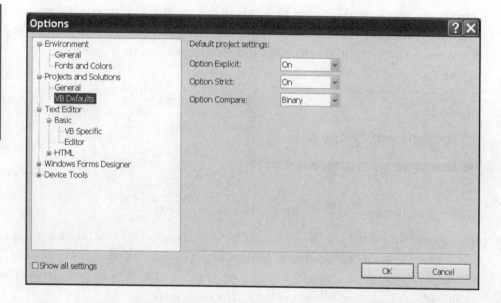

➤   As in VBA, you can set *Option Explicit* to ON (which forces you to declare your variables to be of a certain type)

➤   Also as in VBA, you can set *Option Compare* to *Text* (which makes String searches case-insensitive) versus *Binary*.

➤   *Option Strict* is new in VB.NET. With this *Option* set to ON, VSTO requires explicit conversions for all narrowing conversions that could result in data loss, such as converting from *Double* to *Integer*. This setting is optional and requires more work for you. But it is worth the price, ensuring that you don't perform any unsafe type conversions.

➤   *Option Base 1* is removed from VB.NET (which sets the first element for arrays to 1 instead of 0, see 6.1). This option is no longer valid!

Table 33

Differences
in Options
statements
between
VBA and
VSTO

VB	VB.NET	Illegal if set to ON
Option Explicit	Option **Explicit**	~~Dim X~~
Option Compare	Option **Compare**	
Option Base	–	
–	Option **Strict**	~~Dim X As Integer, Y As Long _~~ ~~X = Y~~
Defaults:	*Tools → Options →* *Project and Solutions →* *VB Defaults*	

Instead of enforcing these settings globally for the entire project, you can also set them individually for certain files by typing "Option ..." on the first line – preceding any declarations or *Imports* statements at the head of the file.

With *Option Strict* set to ON (which is the default), you are telling VB.NET not to perform narrowing conversion, which means casting a variable that is too large for its holder (say, converting from *Long* to *Integer*). In order to perform such a conversion, you must use conversion functions to inform VB.NET that you are aware of the danger. Widening conversion, on the other hand, is always permissible in VB.NET.

Table 34	Functions	Convert Class
Conversion functions in VB.NET	CStr()	Convert.ToString()
	CInt()	Convert.ToInteger()
	CSgl()	Convert.ToSingle()
	And many more	...

Special reference should be made to the function *CType()*. This function allows us to temporarily convert a variable of one *Reference* type (usually *Object*) into another *Reference* type (say, *Worksheet*). Because of *Option Strict*, a variable of the type *Object* cannot be automatically coerced into a more specific object type – unless we use the *CType()* statement.

Remember the case (see 0) where a button's click event provided information about the *sender* (which is of the *Object* type)? In order to find out what is on the face of the button (which is the Button's *Text* property), we need to convert the more general *Object* type of sender into the more specific *Button* type of this entity before we can use its *Text* property:

```
sVar = CType(sender, Button).Text
```

One more issue related to *Option Strict*: Because its default setting is ON, all objects are early-bound by default. Early-Binding means that our code is checked at compile-time (before run-time errors can occur) to determine whether a certain object has the properties and methods used in code; consequently, we get help when typing a period after the object's name in the form of a list of methods (*IntelliSense*). If *Option Strict* is set to OFF, however, late-binding kicks in, so our code is not checked until run-time, which may cause run-time errors. It is clear that neither *IntelliSense* nor compile-time syntax checking are possible in this latter case.

5.1.4 Strings

Handling text requires a good arsenal of tools. I will be brief on this issue. VB.NET provides three powerful classes for manipulating text:

 Char Class – deals with individual characters.

In VB, characters were just strings, albeit one-character strings – not so in VB.NET. This is great if you want to validate user-supplied keystrokes by checking whether a character is a special character, a digit, or a letter, etc. With *Option Strict* ON, you must convert a *String* type such as "A" into a *Character* type by using *CChar()*, before you can test it with a method such as *IsDigit()* (provided by the *Char* class).

There are two versions of this method. The *Char.IsDigit(char)* acts on a character variable, whereas the *Char.IsDigit(string, n)* acts on the nth character of the specified string. In addition, the *Char Class* has other useful methods such as *IsLetter()*, *IsLower()*, *IsUpper()*, and *IsNumber()*. And then there are the well-known methods *ToString()*, *ToLower()*, and *ToUpper()*.

String Class – handles fixed-length strings that do not need editing.

The class has some important properties. The *Length* property returns the number of characters in a string. The *Chars* property holds an array of all the characters in a string, starting at index 0, so you can loop through all its elements (for instance, when you want to check them individually).

There are also numerous, powerful methods. The methods *Replace()*, *Concat()*, *Join()*, *Remove()*, *Insert()*, and *SubString()* all return a new, separate string. (Remember, there is no direct editing in this class.) The method *Split()* returns an array. And of course, there is an equivalent for VB's *InStr()* method: *String.IndexOf()* finds the position of a substring in a larger string.

StringBuilder Class – stores dynamic strings and can manipulate faster than the *String* class. However, you must import *System.Text* first (or use the longer address) before you create a new instance of the class: *Dim txt As New StringBuilder*. Its methods – such as *Append()*, *Insert()*, *Remove()*, *Replace()* – do not return a new, separate string but act directly on the string they are applied to. In other words, they are methods, not functions.

Strings might behave like *Value* types, but they are actually *Reference* types. As a consequence, you should be able to use the *System.String* class' functions – such as *SubString()* to extract parts of a string (something you used to do in VBA with the functions *Left()*, *Mid()*, and *Right()*).

Table 35 *System.String* Class Functions	System String	Examples of String Functions
	.Length	Dim str As String str = InputBox("Type") If str.**Length** = 0 Then …
	.ToUpper	Dim sState As String = "ma" sState = sState.**ToUpper**
	.Split()	Dim path As String = "c:\...\...\" Dim parts() As String parts = path.**Split**(CChar("\"))
	.Replace()	Dim str As String = "VBA" str = str.**Replace**("VBA", "VB.NET")
	.SubString()	Dim str As String = "VB.NET" str = str.**SubString**(0, 2)

	Char Class	String Class	StringBuilder Class
Table 36 *System.String* Classes	IsDigit()	Replace()	Dim str As New System.Text.StringBuilder
	IsLetter()	Concat()	
	IsNumber()	Join()	Append()
	IsLower()	Remove()	Insert()
	IsUpper()	Insert()	Remove()
		Split()	Replace()
		IndexOf()	

5.1.5 Dates

If you work a lot with dates in Excel, you need to know more about the differences between VB and VB.NET in this respect. In VB, you can use dates as "real" *Dates* and *Times* (say, #1/1/2006# or #1/1/2006 12:00:00#) – or you can use them as *Doubles* (38718 or 38718.5), so that you can perform addition and subtraction operations. In other words, VB was capable of interpreting expressions as implicit *Date* operations.

In VB.NET, on the other hand, you may have to convert dates explicitly by using one of these casting methods: *ToOADate*, *ToOATime*, or *ToOADateTime* – to convert a *Date* value type to a *Double* value type, whereas *FromOADate* would do the opposite (*OA* stands for *OLE Automation* compatible). Fortunately, there is a *DateTime* Class that provides these methods: *Imports System.DateTime*.

There are two different ways of using conversions:

  ➢ Dim dbl As Double = Now().**ToOADate**
  ➢ Dim dbl As Double = **System.DateTime.ToOADate**(Now())

It's a similar story for a *Date* that was supplied as a *String*. You need the class' *Parse()* method, which converts a *String* with date-time information into a *Date* value type – regardless of the format of the date string! The method *ToString()* would do the opposite, but it offers many more alternatives: *ToLongDateString*, *ToLongTimeString*, *ToShortDateString*, *ToShortTimeString*, and *ToUniversalTime*. Again, you can have it two different ways:

  ➢ Dim str As String = Now().**ToString**("MM/dd/yyyy")
  ➢ Dim str As String = **System.DateTime.ToString**(Now())

The *System.DateTime* Class also has properties such as *Date*, *DayOfWeek*, *DayOfYear*, *Hour*, *Minute*, *Second*, *Millisecond*, *Day*, *Month*, and *Year*. These properties speak for themselves and allow you to access specific parts of a given date and time.

5.2   New Arithmetic Operators

In addition to the regular VB operators, VB.NET also accepts syntax shortcuts as found in Java and C^{++}. If you are not familiar with those, you may want to at least know about them, because sometimes they are more convenient.

	VB Operators	VB.NET Extra Operators
Table 37 Differences in Syntax between VB Operators and VB.NET Extra Operators	x = x + y	x += y
	x = x / y	x /= y
	x = x \ y	x \= y
	x = x ^ y	x ^= y
	x = x & y	x &= y

The following code is an example of how these new arithmetic operators can save you some time and space. This code creates some 50 random numbers between 1 and 6, as if you were rolling a dice. Then it calculates the frequency that comes with each of those six numbers. Notice how the new binary operators can come in handy.

Code Example 10: Calculating Frequencies with the Use of Arrays

```
Sub CalcFreq()
    Dim rand As Random = New Random
    Dim arrRnd() As Integer
    Dim arrFreq(6) As Integer
    Dim num As String = InputBox("How many?", , "50")
    ReDim arrRnd(CInt(num) - 1)
    For i As Integer = 0 To UBound(arrRnd)
        Dim rnd As Integer = 1 + rand.Next(6)
        arrRnd(i) = rnd
    Next
    For i As Integer = 0 To UBound(arrRnd)
        arrFreq(arrRnd(i)) += 1
    Next
    Dim txt As String = "Score" & vbTab & "Frequency" & vbCr
    Dim total As Integer
    For i As Integer = 1 To UBound(arrFreq)
        txt &= i & vbTab & arrFreq(i) & vbCr
        total += arrFreq(i)
    Next
    MsgBox(txt & vbCr & "Total Count: " & total)
    If MsgBox("Again?", MsgBoxStyle.YesNo) = MsgBoxResult.Yes Then CalcFreq()
End Sub
```

Each pair of statements shown below is equivalent:

arrFreq(arrRnd(i)) **=** arrFreq(arrRnd(i)) **+** 1	arrFreq(arrRnd(i)) **+=** 1
total **=** total **+** arrFreq(i)	total **+=** arrFreq(i)
txt **=** txt **&** i & vbTab & arrFreq(i)	txt **&=** i & vbTab & arrFreq(i)

5.3   Scope and Control Structures

Most of the control structures have remained the same in VB.NET, so we won't spend time on those here. VSTO still accepts *For-Next*, *Do-Loop*, *If-Then*, *Select-Case*, etc. But something has changed regarding the scope of variables in this respect. In VBA, variables declared anywhere in a procedure are accessible from anywhere inside that procedure and are immediately instantiated, no matter where they were declared in the procedure. In other words, all local variables in VB have *procedure-scope*.

Not so in VB.NET: If a variable is declared inside a code block, you can only access it within the scope of that code block. This is called *block-level scope*. What qualifies as a code block? *For-Next* loops, *Do-Loop* loops, *While-Wend* loops, *If-Then* structures, *Case-Select* structures, or *Try-End* error handlers (see 8.1). For people who always declare variables at the start of procedures, this won't be an issue.

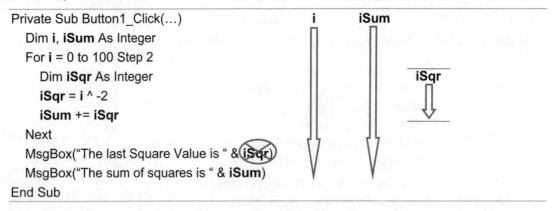

```
Private Sub Button1_Click(…)
    Dim i, iSum As Integer
    For i = 0 to 100 Step 2
        Dim iSqr As Integer
        iSqr = i ^ -2
        iSum += iSqr
    Next
    MsgBox("The last Square Value is " & iSqr)
    MsgBox("The sum of squares is " & iSum)
End Sub
```

The issue of *block-level* scope would naturally affect all cases similar to the following:

```
For Each cell As Excel.Range In ….Range("A1:A10")
For Each WS As Excel.Worksheet In ThisWorkbook.Worksheets
For i As Integer = 0 to 9
Catch ex As Exception                              'See 8.1
```

In this context, we should also mention how VB.NET deals with other scoping options based on different scoping keywords. When we create a sub-class through *inheritance* (see 11.2), the new sub-class gains all the *Public* and *Friend* methods from the base-class, but not what was declared as *Private*. The keywords *Public* and *Friend* make code available to both sub-classes and clients. When you want to exclude clients, use the keyword *Protected* instead.

Table 38

Scope of Keywords as used in VB.NET

Keyword	Scope
Private	Callable within (sub-)class
Friend	Callable within project/component
Public	Callable outside class
Protected	Callable within class/subclasses only
Protected Friend	Callable within project and subclasses

5.4   Case Study: A Rosetta Stone

Figure 25

Message box showing seniority and bonus

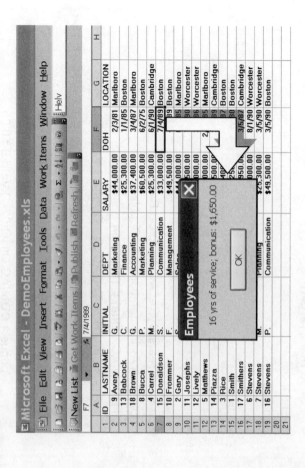

The following code works on a table with information regarding salaries and dates-of-hire for a listing of employees.

Each time the user clicks on a cell with a date in it, the code creates a *Messagebox* that displays the years of seniority plus the bonus that a specific employee is entitled to.

Code Example 11: Calculating Seniority and Bonus Based on Two Cells

VBA Version	VSTO Version

'In Sheet1

```
Private Sub Sheet1_SelectionChange (ByVal _
    Target As Range)

If IsDate(ActiveCell) = True Then
    ShowYears
End If
End Sub
```

'In Module1

```
Sub ShowYears()
Dim iYrs As Integer, bonus As Double
If IsDate(ActiveCell) = True Then
    iYrs = (Now() - ActiveCell) / 365
    Select Case iYrs
        Case 0 To 9
            bonus = ActiveCell.Offset(0, -1) * 0.02
        Case 10 To 19
            bonus = ActiveCell.Offset(0, -1) * 0.05
        Case 20 To 29
            bonus = ActiveCell.Offset(0, -1) * 0.07
        Case Else
```

Public Class Sheet1

```
Private Sub Sheet1_SelectionChange(ByVal Target _
    As Microsoft.Office.Interop.Excel.Range) _
    Handles Me.SelectionChange

If IsDate(Target.Value) = True Then
    ShowYears(Target)
End If
End Sub

End Class
```

Module Module1

```
Sub ShowYears(ByRef AC As Excel.Range)
Dim iYrs As Integer, bonus As Double
If IsDate(AC.Value) = True Then
    iYrs = CInt((Now.ToOADate - CDbl(AC.Value2)) / 365)
    Select Case iYrs
        Case 0 To 9
            bonus = CDbl(AC.Offset(0, -1).Value) * 0.02
        Case 10 To 19
            bonus = CDbl(AC.Offset(0, -1).Value) * 0.05
        Case 20 To 29
            bonus = CDbl(AC.Offset(0, -1).Value) * 0.07
        Case Else
```

VBA Version

```
            bonus = ActiveCell.Offset(0, -1) * 0.1

End Select
MsgBox iYrs & " yrs of service; bonus: " &_
        FormatCurrency(bonus)

    Else

        MsgBox "Not a date"

    End If
End Sub
```

VSTO Version

```
            bonus = CDbl(AC.Offset(0, -1).Value) * 0.1

End Select
MsgBox(iYrs & " yrs of service; bonus: " &_
        FormatCurrency(bonus))

    Else

        MsgBox("Not a date")

    End If
End Sub

End Module
```

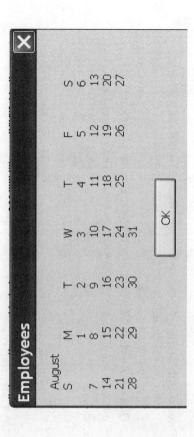

Figure 26

Message box showing calendar for specified month and year

The following code creates a calendar for the month and the year the user specifies through Inputboxes.

The code kicks in whenever the user selects another cell on *Sheet1* while holding the *Ctr* and *Shift* keys.

This code requires extensive date manipulation and uses regular looping techniques. The calendar is displayed in a *MessageBox* (so we don't need to touch *Range* manipulation yet).

VBA Version	VSTO Version

Code Example 12: Displaying a Calendar for a Specific Month and Year

VBA Version	VSTO Version
'Any shortcut created in Excel will do	Public Class Sheet1 Private Sub Sheet1_SelectionChange(ByVal Target As _ Microsoft.Office.Interop.Excel.Range) Handles _ Me.SelectionChange Dim KS As New Microsoft.VisualBasic.Devices.Keyboard If KS.CtrlKeyDown And KS.ShiftKeyDown Then **Calendar**() End Sub End Class

```
Sub Calendar()
    Dim i As Integer, iMonth As Integer, iYear As Integer
    Dim txt As String, dDate As Date
    iMonth = InputBox("Month" , Month(Now()))
    iYear = InputBox("Year" , Year(Now()))
    txt = MonthName(iMonth) & " " & iYear & vbCr

    txt = txt & "S" & vbTab & "M" & vbTab & "T" & vbTab & "W" & _
        vbTab & "T" & vbTab & "F" & vbTab & "S" & vbCr
    dDate = DateSerial(iYear, iMonth, 1)
    dDate = dDate - Weekday(dDate) + 1

    Do
        For i = 0 To 6
            If Month(dDate) = iMonth Then
```

```
Sub Calendar()
    Dim i, iMonth, iYear As Integer
    Dim txt As String, dDate As Date
    iMonth = CInt(InputBox("Month" , , Month(Now()).ToString))
    iYear = CInt(InputBox("Year" , , Year(Now()).ToString))
    txt = MonthName(iMonth) & " " & iYear & vbCr

    txt & = "S" & vbTab & "M" & vbTab & "T" & vbTab & "W" & _
        vbTab & "T" & vbTab & "F" & vbTab & "S" & vbCr
    dDate = DateSerial(iYear, iMonth, 1)
    dDate = System.DateTime.FromOADate(CInt(dDate.ToOADate) - _
        Weekday(dDate) + 1)

    Do
        For i = 0 To 6
            If Month(dDate) = iMonth Then
```

VBA Version	VSTO Version

`txt = txt & Day(dDate) & vbTab`
 	
`        Else`
`            txt = txt & vbTab`
`        End If`
`        dDate = dDate + 1`
 	
`    Next`
`    txt = txt & vbCr`
`Loop While Month(dDate) = iMonth`
`MsgBox txt`
 	
`End Sub`
	`txt = txt & _`
	`        Microsoft.VisualBasic.DateAndTime. Day(dDate) & _`
	`            vbTab`
	
	`        Else`
	`            txt = txt & vbTab`
	`        End If`
	`        dDate = _`
	`            System.DateTime.FromOADate(CInt(dDate.ToOADate) _`
	`                + 1)`
	
	`    Next`
	`    txt = txt & vbCr`
	`Loop While Month(dDate) = iMonth`
	`MsgBox(txt)`
	
	`End Sub`

6   Array Changes

6.1   Regular Arrays

All arrays in VB.NET are zero-based; in other words, there is no *Option Base* anymore — nor can you say *Dim arr(5 To 10)*. You won't have any problems migrating array code from VBA to VSTO if you never used *Option Base* statements or *To* statements. If you did, however, you must rework your code in one of the following ways:

➤ Add one element to all arrays in order to maintain an *Option Base* of 1. This creates an extra, empty slot at index 0, but you can still keep your loops running from 1 to n.

➤ Make all indexes zero-based — which is more work, but it is the only solution if you ever used *LBound()* and *UBound()*. In VB.NET, you can still use *UBound()*, but since an array is an instance of the class *System.Array*, you can also use its property *Length* (the total number of elements in all dimensions), or its functions *GetUpperBound(0)* and *GetLength(0)-1* (but in these two cases, you must specify inside the parentheses which dimension you are talking about, starting at 0 and not at 1, as you would in VBA).

In VSTO, an array is still a bit of a hybrid. Because there is a *Class* behind it, you may use the *New* keyword to create an instance of a class. However, the older VBA version (without the use of the *New* keyword) is still valid — in spite of the fact that an array variable is of the *Reference* type.

The following are all legal array creations in VSTO.

```
Dim arr(4) As Integer
Dim arr() As Integer = New Integer() {}
Dim arr() As Integer = {1,2,3,4,5}
Dim arr() As Integer = New Integer() {1,2,3,4,5}
```

6.1.1   One-Dimensional Arrays

Let us start with the simplest kind of array there is: a one-dimensional array. There are at least three key issues here:

➤ An array that has been declared has not necessarily been created. Declaration and creation can be done in two steps or can be combined in one step. Once creation has taken effect, the array exists and has a certain length — which can be zero.

➤ What does an array with a length > 0 contain in each of its elements? That depends on how the array was created. An array may have been initialized with specific values at creation time; initialization is usually done inside braces: {...}. If nothing has been placed inside the braces, each element just contains a default value — which is 0 for numeric types, *False* for *Booleans*,

Nothing for *References*, or an empty *String*. Needless to say, initialized values as well as default values can be altered later on in code.

➤ The length of an existing array can be changed by using a *ReDim* statement. But there is at least one *ReDim* change in VSTO: Not only can you use *ReDim* after dynamic array declarations – *Dim arr()* – but also after static declarations – *Dim arr(n)* –, which latter option was not possible in VBA. If you also use the *Preserve* keyword – *ReDim Preserve arr(n)* – don't forget that only the last dimension can be resized – just like it used to be in VBA. More on this in the next chapter.

The following overview shows you a collection of array statements legal in VSTO. Declaration and creation are either split or combined. Values are either initialized or left as defaults. And the *New* keyword is either used or left out. Take your pick of what you want to use in your own projects.

Table 39

Overview of legal array statements in VSTO

		Array declaration	Array creation	Array Length	Array Values
Default values	Split	Dim arr() As Integer	ReDim arr(4)	5	0,0,0,0,0
		Dim arr As Integer	arr = New Integer(4) {}		
		Dim arr As Integer()	arr = New Integer(4) {}		
		Dim arr As Integer()	arr = New Integer() {}	0	–
	Combined	Dim arr(4) As Integer		5	0,0,0,0,0
		Dim arr() As Integer = New Integer(4) {}			
		Dim arr() As Integer = New Integer() {}		0	–
Initialized values	Split	Dim arr() As Integer	ReDim arr(4) : arr(0)=1 : arr(1)=2 …	5	1,2,3,4,5
		Dim arr As Integer	arr = New Integer(4) {1,2,3,4,5}		
		Dim arr As Integer()	arr = New Integer() {1,2,3,4,5}		
	Combined	Dim arr() As Integer = {1, 2, 3, 4, 5}		5	1,2,3,4,5
		Dim arr As Integer() = New Integer() {1, 2, 3, 4, 5}			
		Dim arr As Integer() = New Integer(4) {1, 2, 3, 4, 5}			

6.1.2   Two-Dimensional Arrays

The previous arrays are all one-dimensional. What about two-dimensional ones? There are basically two different kinds:

➢ *Rectangular* arrays are really two-dimensional. The length of the second dimension is specified after a comma; so *arr(1,2)* has two elements in the first dimension and three elements in the second dimension. They are called rectangular because the number of "rows" is identical for each "column", and the reverse. An Excel spreadsheet is a good example of a rectangular array.

➢ *Jagged* arrays are not really two-dimensional; however, they constitute an array of arrays – actually a 1-D array of multiple 1-D arrays. As a consequence, each element in the main array can hold an array of varying length. This will save you memory space when the number of elements in the second dimension varies.

Table 40 Comparison of *Rectangular* and *Jagged* array codes	Type	Code for two dimensions	Results
	Rectangular	Dim arr(**1, 2**) As Integer	arr(0, 0) is 0 arr(1, 2) is 0
	Rectangular	Dim arr(**,**) As Integer = {{1,2,3},{11,12,13}}	arr(0, 0) is 1 arr(1, 2) is 13
	Jagged	Dim arr(**1**)() As Integer arr(0) = New Integer() {1, 2, 3, 4} arr(1) = New Integer() {11, 22}	arr(0) (0) is 1 arr(1) (1) is 22
	Jagged	Dim arr()() As Integer arr = New Integer(**1**)() {} arr(0) = New Integer() {1, 2, 3, 4} arr(1) = New Integer() {11, 22}	arr(0) (3) is 4 arr(1) (1) is 22

Employee timesheets could be used as an example of a *jagged* array because employees usually have different numbers of timesheets. However, I used another example in the following case: a *jagged* array for sales figures on each day of the year. These sales figures are based on a random number between 0 and 1 multiplied by 1000. The end result is an array of 12 months, with each month holding a sub-array for the number of days in that specific month.

Code Example 13: Creating a Jagged Array (1-D Array with 1-D Subarrays)

```
Sub Sales()
    Dim daily()() As Double = New Double(11)() {}
    Dim rand As Random = New Random
    For i As Integer = 0 To 11
        Dim days As Integer = DateTime.DaysInMonth(Year(Now()), i + 1)
        daily(i) = New Double(days - 1) {}
        For j As Integer = 0 To UBound(daily(i))
            Dim rnd As Double = rand.NextDouble() * 1000
            daily(i)(j) = rnd
```

```
            Dim txt As String = "On " & i + 1 & "/" & j + 1 & ": " & FormatCurrency(daily(i)(j))
            System.Diagnostics.Debug.Print(txt)
        Next
    Next i
    Stop 'Check here the Immediate Window
End Sub
```

There are also arrays with more than two dimensions. If you need a three-dimensional array, use something like *arr(1,2,3)*. But be aware of the following: *ReDim* can add new elements to an array, but it cannot add new dimensions. A solution for this limitation would be to declare a second array with an extra dimension and then copy the first array into the second array.

Code Example 14: Adding a New Dimension to an Array

```
Dim arr1(4, 4) As Integer
Dim arr2(4, 4, 4) As Integer
'Fill arr1 here
For dim1 As Integer = 0 to arr1.GetLength(0)-1
    For dim2 As Integer = 0 to arr1.GetLength(1)-1
        arr2(dim1, dim2, 0) = arr1(dim1, dim2)
        'Fill the third dimension of arr2 here
    Next
Next
```

And then we have the *Variant* problem when migrating from VBA to VSTO. What would you do if you had used arrays in VBA whose type was *Variant* or that were not declared to be any type (which made them of the *Variant* type anyway)? Ask yourself, "What are the types that have been stored in the array?", and then choose the most specific super-class that can represent all of them (such as *Double* for *Single*, *Integer*, and *Short*). You may end up with the super-class of all classes – *Object* – or you could just decide on a "cheaper" type – say, *String* – and convert the other types directly by using a conversion function such as *CStr()*. More on this issue later (see 6.3).

I also have some good news for you: Sure enough, arrays are based on a *Class*. And this class, *System.Array*, has some powerful methods and functions to offer, such as *Sort()*, *Reverse()*, *Copy()*, *BinarySearch()*, and *IndexOf()*. All you have to do is call the class' methods and apply them to your array.

Code Example 15: Using Array Class Methods

```
Dim arr1() As Short = {3, 2, 1}
Dim arr2(2) As Short
Array.Sort(arr1)
Array.Copy(arr1, arr2, arr1.Length)
For Each item As Short In arr2
    MessageBox.Show("Element: " & item)
Next
Dim found As Integer = Array.BinarySearch(arr2, CShort(3))
MsgBox("3 is at position: " & found)
```

6.1.3 ArrayLists

In spite of all these powerful methods, arrays are still static structures – which means it is time-consuming to resize them or to insert and delete elements. And that's where VB.NET comes to our rescue again with another, even more powerful class: *ArrayList*. This class offers a dynamic structure that can grow and shrink automatically as you add or delete elements.

It is possible, though, to set the *ArrayList*'s capacity ahead of time. If you don't want to do so, VB.NET will automatically reserve 16 elements, and then double the capacity whenever needed. However, it doesn't decrease the capacity when you remove items.

Code Example 16: Using ArrayList Methods

```
Dim arrList As New ArrayList
arrList.Capacity = 100
If Not arrList.Contains("Two") Then arrList.Add("Two")
arrList.Insert(0, "One")
arrList.Remove("Two")
arrList.RemoveAt(arrList.Count-1)
```

6.2   Structured Arrays

What VBA used to do with the *Type* keyword, VSTO does with the *Structure* keyword (see also 9.2). As to *Structures*, the keyword *Dim* is equivalent to *Public* – otherwise, you must use *Private*.

Well, *Structures* can be used in arrays as well (just the way you did in VBA with *Custom Types*). In the following example, we use an array of "Check" *Structures*.

Code Example 17: Creating a Structured Array

```
Structure Check
    Dim chNum As Integer
    Dim chDate As Date
    Dim chAmount As Single
    Dim chTo As String
End Structure
Dim Checks(9) As Check
For i As Integer = 0 To Checks.Length-1
    Checks(i).chNum = …
    …
Next
Function GetCheckInfo(ByVal ID As Integer) As Check
    Return Checks(ID)
End Function
Dim Check5 As Check = GetCheckInfo(4)
End Structure

Next

End Function
```

In the above case, how would you easily spot duplicate entries of checks? Well, all data types expose the *Equals*() method, which is especially useful when the data type is a *Structure*, because you do not have to compare the individual fields for each check.

```
For i As Integer = 0 To Checks.length-2
    For j As Integer = i+1 To Checks.Length-1
        If Checks(i).Equals(Checks(j)) Then ...
    Next
Next
```

Given the fact that you create arrays of structures, it won't be a surprise that you can also place an array inside a structure. Say, you want to specify the names of up to five persons who gave their OK for issuing the check.

```
Structure Check
    Dim chNum As Integer
    Dim chDate As Date
    Dim chAmount As Single
    Dim chTo As String
    Dim chOK(4) As String
End Structure
```
MsgBox("The 3rd OK for check 5: " & Checks(4).chOK(2))

I think at this point you have enough cues as to how to handle situations like these in your VSTO code.

6.3   What happened to Variant Arrays?

Since Excel spreadsheets basically have a two-dimensional configuration, I personally loved the fact that you could use *Variant* arrays in VBA to temporarily "store" sections of a spreadsheet (such as *Range*, *Selection*, and *CurrentRegion*). I am not speaking of an array declared to be of the *Variant* type, but I am referring to a *Variant* that can hold anything, including an array of a two-dimensional range of cell values.

Table 41 Comparing the old situation in VBA ...	The "old" situation in VBA	
	Array that holds items of the *Variant* type.	Variable of the *Variant* type that can hold anything, including arrays.
	Dim arr() As **Variant**	Dim arr As **Variant** **arr = Selection**

Since there is no *Variant* value type anymore in VB.NET, you may wonder whether you can still employ a similar handy feature. The answer is a cautious Yes.

Do you remember that *Object* has replaced *Variant*? So, we should be able to do the same tricks with the *Object* type as we used to do with the *Variant* type. But I must warn you: There is a bit more conversion trouble when *Option Strict* is ON (and that should be the case if at all possible).

Table 42 ... with the new situation in VBA	The "new" situation in VSTO	
	Dim arr() As **Object**	Dim arr As **Object**
		~~arr = Application.Selection.Value2~~
	Array that holds items of the *Object* type.	Variable of the *Object* type that can hold anything, including arrays.

Let's go back to the distinction between early-binding and late-binding (see 5.1.3). Since the *Object* type can hold any value type and can refer to any kind of object, it is an example of late-binding, and therefore doesn't allow for compile-time checking.

Table 43 Comparing early binding to late binding	**Early-binding**	**Late-binding**
	Dim oObj As **myClass**	Dim oObj As **Object**
	Allows for compile-time checking	Waits for run-time checking
	Faster than late-binding	More error prone
	No problem with Option Strict ON	Option Strict ON requires *CType()*

Imagine that you want your users to select a range of cells, multiply its values with a certain factor, and then allow them to have the option of setting the range back to what it was before – something like an *Undo* operation. I always found it easy to store the original range in an array, and then use this array to set the range back to its original values, if so desired. The problem is that VBA's *Selection* object had *Value* as a default property, whereas VSTO's *Selection* doesn't.

Table 44 Using arrays to undo *Range* changes		**VBA**	**VSTO**
	Store in array	Dim oOld As **Variant** oOld = Selection	Dim oOld As **Object** oOld = **Application**.Selection.**Value2**
	Undo from array	Selection = oOld	**Application**.Selection.**Value2** = oOld

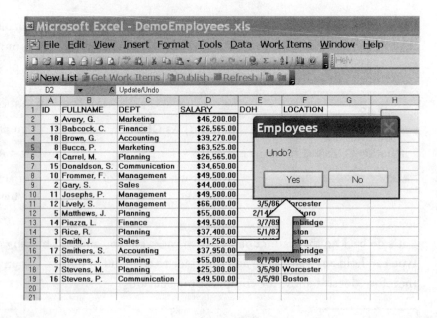

Figure 27

Message box showing option to undo range changes by restoring the range from an array

The following code should do the job.

1. Store the range in an *Object*'s array.

2. Change something inside the range.

3. Restore the range from the array.

Code Example 18: Undoing Range Changes by Using an Array

```
Module myModule

    Dim thisWB As Excel.Workbook = CType(Globals.ThisWorkbook, _
        Excel.Workbook)

    Sub UpdateAndUndo()
        Dim SEL As Excel.Range = CType(thisWB.Application.InputBox _
            ("Select Range", , "a1", , , , , 8), Excel.Range)
        Dim oOld As Object = SEL.Value2
        Dim sFactor As String = InputBox("Multiply by", , "1.05")
        For Each cell As Excel.Range In SEL
            If IsNumeric(cell.Value) Then cell.Value = Val(cell.Value) * Val(sFactor)
        Next
        If MsgBox("Undo?", MsgBoxStyle.YesNo) = MsgBoxResult.Yes Then
            SEL.Value2 = oOld
        End If
    End Sub

End Module
```

One of the advantages of using *Variant* arrays in VBA is/was the fact that manipulating an array is much faster than manipulating a range of cells. So it would be nice to actually create two (yes, two) temporary arrays:

> One array for "undo" options (as we did previously)

> Another array for manipulating data (because array manipulation is faster than range manipulation)

However, in the second array, we really get into problems in how to address the individual elements in an *Object* that wasn't declared an array immediately, but rather became one afterwards (so-called late-binding). And remember, with *Option Strict* ON, late-binding causes problems.

So I would suggest the simplest and easiest solution: Store this code in a new module and set – with pain in your heart – *Option Strict* to OFF for this single module only.

Table 45 Comparing Option Strict On code with Option Strict Off code	Module1 (old)	Module2 (new)
	Option Strict **On** Module **Mod1**	Option Strict **Off** Module **Mod2**
	Sub UpdateAndUndo() 　'Store Range in Array 　'Do something in **Range** 　'Restore Range from Array	Sub UpdateAndUndo() 　'Store Range in **2** Arrays 　'Do something in **Array1** 　'Fill Array1 back in Range 　'Undo Range with Array2
	End Sub	End Sub
	End Module	End Module

If you want to study the more long-winded code for performing the above procedure, here it is (by the way, I assume the 2-D array only covers one column of values – otherwise you'd need a loop inside a loop):

1. Store the *Range* in two *Objects* as an array.

2. Store *array1* in object *oNew* (for *Range* manipulation).

3. Use *array2* in object *oOld* (for *Range* restoration).

Code Example 19: Using Arrays to Manipulate and Restore Ranges

```
Option Strict Off

Module Module2

    Dim thisWB As Excel.Workbook = CType(Globals.ThisWorkbook, _
        Excel.Workbook)

    Sub UpdateAndUndo()
        Dim SEL As Excel.Range = _
            thisWB.Application.InputBox ("Select Range", , "A1", , , , , 8)
```

```
        Dim sFactor As String = InputBox("Multiply by", , "1.05")
        Dim oOld As Object = SEL.Value2
        Dim oNew As Object = SEL.Value2
        For i As Integer = 1 To UBound(oNew, 1)
            If IsNumeric(oNew(i, 1)) Then oNew(i, 1) = Val(oNew(i, 1)) * _
                Val(sFactor)
        Next
        SEL.Value2 = oNew
        If MsgBox("Undo?", MsgBoxStyle.YesNo) = MsgBoxResult.Yes Then
            SEL.Value2 = oOld
        End If
    End Sub

End Module
```

And then there are arrays passed in parameters. The following code has a custom method called *AddNames()*; this method accepts arrays and then displays each element through a *MsgBox()*. Another custom method, named *Test()*, calls the previous method and passes a *String* array to the method. The keyword here is *ParamArray*.

Code Example 20: Using Arrays as Parameters

```
Option Strict On

Module Module1
    Dim arrNames() As String = {"Mary", "John"}

    Sub AddNames(ByVal ParamArray arr() As Object)
        For Each i As Object In arr
            MsgBox(i.ToString)
        Next
    End Sub

    Sub Test()
        AddNames(arrNames)
    End Sub

End Module
```

6.4   Case Study: A Rosetta Stone

Figure 28

Sorting sheets in alphabetical order

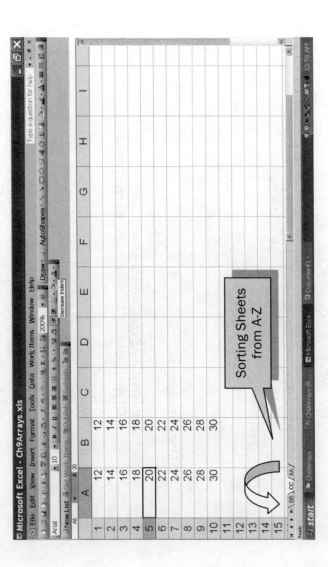

The following code stores the name of each worksheet in a 1-D array, sorts the names alphabetically inside the array, and then moves the worksheets around according to the sorted order in the array.

All of this is done without any screen updating. But be aware that this procedure triggers *Activate* events in all sheets, so code inside those events will run as well.

Because the sorting is case sensitive, the array holds only the lowercase versions of the worksheet names. First we make sure that all Worksheets do have a customized name to begin with.

Code Example 21: Moving Sheets Around in an Alphabetical Order

VBA Version	VSTO Version

Private Sub Workbook_Open()
 	
  Sheets(1).Name = "BB"
  Sheets(2).Name = "CC"
  Sheets(3).Name = "AA"
  If MsgBox("Sort the sheets?", vbYesNo) = vbYes Then _
    MoveSheets()
End Sub
	Public Class ThisWorkbook
	
	  Private Sub ThisWorkbook_Startup(ByVal sender As Object, _
	    ByVal e As System.EventArgs) Handles Me.Startup
	    CType(Me.Sheets(1), Excel.Worksheet).Name = "BB"
	    CType(Me.Sheets(2), Excel.Worksheet).Name = "CC"
	    CType(Me.Sheets(3), Excel.Worksheet).Name = "AA"
	    If MsgBox("Sort the sheets?", MsgBoxStyle.YesNo) = _
	      MsgBoxResult.Yes Then MoveSheets()
	  End Sub
	
	End Class

'In Module	Module myModule

Sub MoveSheets()
 	
  Application.ScreenUpdating = False
 	
  Dim n As Integer, i As Integer, j As Integer
  Dim arr() As String, temp As String
  n = WorkSheets.Count
	Dim thisWB As Excel.Workbook = _
	    CType(Globals.ThisWorkbook, Excel.Workbook)
	
	Sub MoveSheets()
	
	  Dim **AP** As Excel.Application = Ctype(**thisWB**.Application, _
	    Excel.Application)
	  AP.ScreenUpdating = False
	
	  Dim I, j As Integer, **n** As Integer = **thisWB**.Worksheets.Count – 1
	  Dim arr(**n**) As String, temp As String

VBA Version	VSTO Version

`ReDim arr(1 To n)`
`Dim AW As Worksheet`
`Set AW = ActiveWorksheet`
`For i = 1 To n`
 	
`    arr(i) = LCase(WorkSheets(i).Name)`
`Next`
`For i = 1 To UBound(arr) - 1`
`    For j = i + 1 To UBound(arr)`
`        If arr(i) > arr(j) Then temp = arr(i) : arr(i) = arr(j) : arr(j) = temp`
`    Next`
`Next`
`For i = 1 To UBound(arr)`
 	
`    WorkSheets(arr(i)).Move  WorkSheets(i)`
`Next i`
`AW.Activate`
`Application.ScreenUpdating = True`
`End Sub`
	`Dim AW As Excel.Worksheet = CType(thisWB.ActiveSheet, _`
	`    Excel.Worksheet)`
	`For I = 0 To n`
	`    Dim WS As Excel.Worksheet = _`
	`        CType(thisWB.Worksheets(I + 1), Excel.Worksheet)`
	`    arr(i) = LCase(WS.Name)`
	`Next`
	`For I = 0 To Ubound(arr) – 1`
	`    For j = I + 1 To arr.GetUpperbound(0)`
	`        If arr(i) > arr(j) Then temp = arr(i) : arr(i) = arr(j) : arr(j) = temp`
	`    Next`
	`Next`
	`For I = 0 To Ubound(arr)`
	`    Dim WS1 As Excel.Worksheet = _`
	`        CType(thisWB.Worksheets(I + 1), Excel.Worksheet)`
	`    Dim WS2 As Excel.Worksheet = _`
	`        CType(thisWB.Worksheets(arr(i)), Excel.Worksheet)`
	`    WS2.Move(WS1)`
	`Next`
	`AW.Activate()`
	`AP.ScreenUpdating = True`
	`End Sub`
	
	`End Module`

Figure 29

Single column range of entries sorted into a unique list for the user

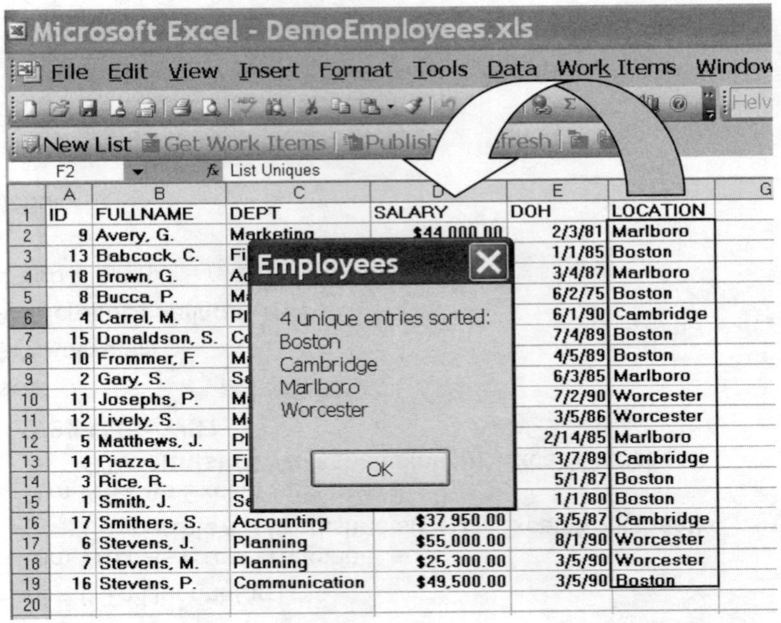

The following code lets the users select a one-column range of entries and then creates a sorted list of unique items in this range.

This time, we use the *ArrayList* class, because it has painless methods of adding and removing items.

The result of this manipulation inside the *ArrayList* is displayed in a *MessageBox* – alphabetically listing the unique entries as found in the selected range.

VBA Version

VSTO Version

Code Example 22: Creating a Sorted List of Unique Items from a Selected Range

'In Module

```
Sub ListUniques()
    Dim SEL As Range, arr() As String, I As Long, j As Long, temp _
        As String, bDup As Boolean
    Set SEL = Application.InputBox("Select Range", , , , , , 8)
```

```
Module myModule

    Dim thisWB As Excel.Workbook = Ctype(Globals.ThisWorkbook, _
        Excel.Workbook)

    Sub ListUniques()
        Dim SEL As Excel.Range = Ctype(thisWB.Application.InputBox _
            ("Select Range", "A1", , , , , 8), Excel.Range)
```

VBA Version

```vba
If SEL.Columns.Count > 1 Then MsgBox ("Only 1 column"): _
    Exit Sub
ReDim arr(0): arr(0) = SEL.Cells(1, 1)
For I = 2 To SEL.Count
    bDup = False
    For j = 0 To UBound(arr)
        If arr(j) = SEL.Cells(I, 1) Then bDup = True: Exit For
    Next j
    If bDup = False Then
        ReDim Preserve arr(UBound(arr) + 1)
        arr(UBound(arr)) = SEL.Cells(I, 1)
    End If
Next i
For I = 0 To UBound(arr, 1) - 1
    For j = I + 1 To UBound(arr, 1)
        If Lcase(arr(i)) > Lcase(arr(j)) Then
            temp = arr(i): arr(i) = arr(j): arr(j) = temp
        End If
    Next j
Next i
temp = (UBound(arr) + 1) & " unique entries sorted: " & vbCr
For I = 0 To UBound(arr)
    temp = temp & arr(i) & vbCr
Next
MsgBox (temp)
End Sub
```

VSTO Version

```vb
If SEL.Columns.Count > 1 Then MsgBox("Only 1 column") : _
    Exit Sub
Dim arrList As New ArrayList
For I As Integer = 1 To SEL.Rows.Count
    arrList.Add(Ctype(SEL(I, 1), Excel.Range).Value2)
Next
arrList.Sort()
For I As Integer = (arrList.Count – 1) To 1 Step -1
    If arrList.Item(i).ToString = arrList.Item(I – 1).ToString _
        Then arrList.RemoveAt(i)
Next

Dim temp As String = CStr(arrList.Count) & " unique entries _
    sorted: " & vbCr
For I As Integer = 0 To arrList.Count – 1
    temp = temp & arrList.Item(i).ToString & vbCr
Next
MsgBox(temp)
End Sub

End Module
```

From VBA to VSTO: Is Excel's New Engine for You?

Figure 30

Creating a *jagged* array of randomly generated bank credits for 15 days

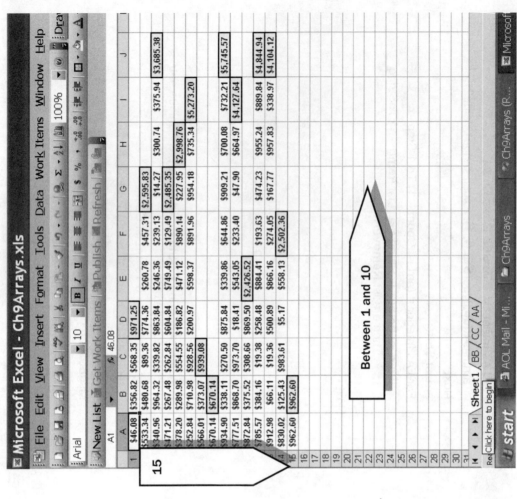

The following code creates a new sheet with a *jagged* array of randomly generated bank checks for 15 days.

The main array contains 15 elements (say, 15 days or 15 accounts). Each element holds a subarray that has a number of elements based on a random number between 1 and 10. Each element in this subarray contains a check amount generated as a random number between 0 and 1 multiplied by 1000.

Once the array of arrays has been created, all its values will be printed out on the new sheet in currency format, including a total amount in red per subarray at the end of each row.

Code Example 23: Creating a Jagged Array of Bank Checks for 15 Days

VBA Version	VSTO Version

VBA Version

```
'In Module1

Sub JaggedArray()
Dim arr(14) As Variant, tempArr As Variant, i As Integer, j As Integer, _
    ub As Integer, NS As Worksheet

For i = 0 To UBound(arr)
    ub = Rnd() * 10
    arr(i) = Array()
    tempArr = arr(i)
    ReDim tempArr(ub)
    For j = 0 To ub
        tempArr(j) = Format(Rnd() * 100, "$0.00")

    Next j
    arr(i) = tempArr
Next i
Set NS = Worksheets.Add

Cells().Clear
For i = 0 To UBound(arr)

    For j = 0 To UBound(arr(i))
```

VSTO Version

```
Module Module1

    Dim thisWB As Excel.Workbook = _
        CType(Globals.ThisWorkbook, Excel.Workbook)

    Sub JaggedArray()
    Dim arr()() As Double = New Double(14)() {}
    Dim rand As Random = New Random

    For i As Integer = 0 To 14
        Dim ub As Integer = 1 + rand.Next(9)
        arr(i) = New Double(ub) {}

        For j As Integer = 0 To ub
            Dim check As Double = rand.NextDouble() * 1000
            arr(i)(j) = check
        Next j

    Next i
    Dim NS As Excel.Worksheet = _
        CType(thisWB.Worksheets. Add(), Excel.Worksheet)
    NS.Cells().Clear()
    For i As Integer = 0 To UBound(arr)
        Dim n As Integer
        For j As Integer = 0 To UBound(arr(i))
```

From VBA to VSTO: Is Excel's New Engine for You?

83

VBA Version	VSTO Version
Cells(i + 1, j + 1).Value = arr(i)(j)	CType(**NS**.Cells(i + 1, j + 1), Excel.Range).Value2 = _ FormatCurrency(arr(i)(j))
Next j	n = j Next j
Cells(i + 1, j + 1).FormulaR1C1 = "=sum(RC[" & -j & "]:RC[-1])"	CType(**NS**.Cells(i + 1, n + 1), Excel.Range).FormulaR1C1 = _ "=sum(RC[" & -n & "]:RC[-1])"
Cells(i + 1, j + 1).Interior.Color = vbRed	CType(**NS**.Cells(i + 1, n + 1), Excel.Range).Interior.Color = _ RGB(255, 0, 0)
Next i Cells().EntireColumn.AutoFit End Sub	Next i **NS**.Cells().EntireColumn.AutoFit() End Sub
	End Module

7   Forms Instead of UserForms

7.1   Form Class

In VB.NET, forms are treated as classes. That wasn't really the case in VBA, where you could make the following statement: *UserForm1.Show*. By doing so, you didn't really create a *UserForm* object, but the *VB Runtime* created the instance on your behalf in the background; it was a default instance. On the other hand, you could have created an instance yourself – an explicit instance, so to speak – by using the following statement: *Dim myForm As New UserForm1*. Then you could interact with this specific instance of the *UserForm* by using the code: *myForm.Show*.

The problem is, however, that you could make a mistake and instead type: *UserForm1.Show*. As a consequence, the displayed *UserForm* would be the default instance – not the explicit instance you had created, now needlessly floating around in memory. What's the underlying problem here? There is a mix-up between a *UserForm* object and a *UserForm* class, between an instance of the class and the class itself.

This is not the case in VB.NET: *UserForms* are gone, replaced by *Forms* – and *Forms* are treated as real classes. *Form1* is actually a subclass of the class *System.Windows.Forms*. This is achieved by the following statement: *Inherits System.Windows.Forms*. Thanks to this line, the new form inherits all the properties, methods, and events of this base class.

```
Imports System.Windows
Imports System.ComponentModel
Imports System.Drawing

Public Class Form1
    Inherits System.Windows.Forms


    Protected Sub Button1_Click(...) Handles Button1
            MsgBox(Me.Text)
    End Sub
End Class
```

Being a class, *Form1* also has a *New()* method – a constructor method comparable to the *Class_Initialize* event in VBA. The base-class is known by the keyword *MyBase*, just as the current instance of the class is known by the keyword *Me*. Now we can use the *New()* method to call the constructor in the base-class: *MyBase.New()*. Next it is necessary to make the keyword *Me* and the variable *Form1* both refer to the current form, which is done this way: Form1 = Me. Thanks to the previous line, we can go either way from now on: either Form1.BackColor or Me.BackColor.

The mirror image of the *New()* method is the *Dispose()* method – comparable to the *Form_Unload* or *Class_Terminate* events. When there is need for a clean-up, we call the *Dispose()* method of *MyBase* and of all the components on the form.

Table 46 Directions for creating a Form	**Steps to Take – Creating a Form**
	1. Go to *Project* → *Add Windows Form*. 2. Select *Windows Form* → Name it → Click *Add*. 3. Drag a button from the *Toolbox* onto the *Form*. You could call a new *Class Diagram*: 4. Right-click on the project in the *Solution Explorer*. 5. Select *View Class Diagram*.

To work with your new Form – let's say it is called *Form1* – you really need to create an instance of the class *Form1*, which you can do with these two lines:

```
Dim WF As New Form1
WF.Show()
```

Or you could also say:

```
Dim WF As Form1 = New Form1
WF.Show()
```

In VBA – at least since 2000 – you could show a form as either *vbModal* (for exclusive use) or *vbModeless* (allowing you to switch back and forth between *Form* and *Sheet*). VSTO offers two different methods:

- The *ShowDialog()* method displays a form modally.

- The *Show()* method, on the other hand, displays a modeless form – which unfortunately moves to the background when the Excel document is activated again.

Table 47 Comparing Form1 code and ThisWorkbook code	**Code at two locations in VSTO**	
	Form1.vb	**ThisWorkbook.vb**

	Public Class **Form1**
	  Public Sub New()
	    InitializeComponent()
	    Me.Cursor = Cursors.Hand
	    Me.Button1.Text = "Close"
	  End Sub
	  Private Sub Button1_Click(…) _
	      Handles Button1.Click
	    Me.Close()
	  End Sub
	End Class
		Public Class ThisWorkbook
		  Private Sub ThisWorkbook_Startup(…) _
		      Handles Me.Startup
		    Dim **WF** As New **Form1**
		    WF.ShowDialog()
		  End Sub
		End Class

You don't really have to worry about the code that regulates the design of the *Form*, because it is automatically generated when you create a Form in the design window. For this purpose, the section called *Form1.Designer.vb* (or whatever name your form bears) is produced. It creates instances of the various controls you have dragged onto the *Form*, including their values, positions, sizes, and so forth.

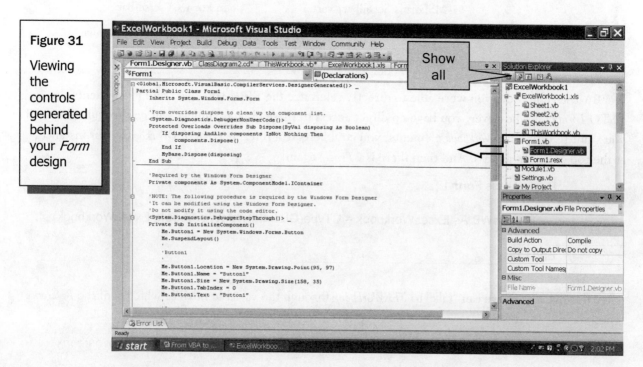

Figure 31

Viewing the controls generated behind your *Form* design

Let's spend some time on the *Form* components that you can drag onto any *Form*.

7.2   Form Elements

UserForms in VBA are based on the *MSForms* type library, whereas *Forms* in VSTO are based on *System.Windows.Forms*. Yet, most of the controls, most of their properties, and most of their events are still the same in both versions. However, some controls have changed names (for instance, *CommandButton* has become *Button*). And, of course, you have many more choices in VSTO! Furthermore, some properties have changed names (e.g., *CommandButton.Caption* has been changed into *Button.Text*) – which is usually an improvement. Finally, some methods have changed – for instance, *ListBox1.AddItem* has become *ListBox.Items.Add()*.

Table 48

Comparing VBA and VSTO control names

VBA Controls (old names)	VSTO Controls (changed names)
MSForms.Frame	...Forms.GroupBox
MSForms.OptionButton	...Forms.RadioButton
MSForms.CommandButton	...Forms.Button
MSForms.TabStrip	...Forms.TabControl

VBA Controls (old names)	VSTO Controls (changed names)
MSForms.MultiPage	...Forms.TabControl
MSForms.Scrollbar (hor.)	...Forms.HscrollBar
MSForms.Scrollbar (vert.)	...Forms.VscrollBar
MSForms.SpinButton	...Forms.DomainUpDown
MSForms.Image	...Forms.PictureBox

In VBA *UserForm* code, you were able to directly reference the *Workbook* object and its elements. In VSTO *Form* code, however, you have no direct access to these objects, unless you go through *Globals*. If you want to deal with *Workbook* elements, you could create a reference to *ThisWorkbook* – for instance, at the top of the *Form* class. And then there is *CType()* again!

```
Public Class Form1

    Dim thisWB As Excel.Workbook = CType(Globals.ThisWorkbook, Excel.Workbook)

End Class
```

After this maneuver, we can "talk" to *ThisWorkbook* through the variable *thisWB*, which is of the *Reference* type.

```
Dim thisWB As Excel.Workbook = CType(Globals.ThisWorkbook, Excel.Workbook)

Private Sub Form1_Load(ByVal sender As System.Object, ByVal e As _
    System.EventArgs) Handles MyBase.Load
    Dim AW As Excel.Worksheet = CType(thisWB.ActiveSheet, Excel.Worksheet)
    AW.Copy(AW)
    Dim AC As Excel.Range = CType(thisWB.Application.ActiveCell, Excel.Range)
    AC.CurrentRegion.Select()
End Sub
```

 Note:

Lighter colored text in code samples indicates code that was automatically inserted by VSTO.

Another issue we should mention is the fact that *Forms* have several new controls that you can just drag onto the *Form* from the *Toolbox*. One of these is the *Tooltip* control in the section *Common Controls*. In other words, there is no *TooltipText* property anymore. Once you drag these kinds of controls – which are basically "invisible" to the user - onto the *Form*, they automatically show up below the *Form* (but you cannot directly drag them to that bottom position).

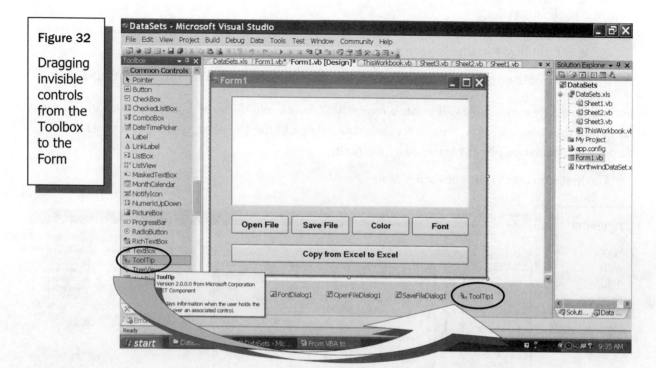

Figure 32

Dragging invisible controls from the Toolbox to the Form

Now you can use this "invisible" *ToolTip* control in your code by using the name of its instance – in this case, *ToolTip1*.

Code Example 24: Implementing Tooltip Information

```
Private Sub Form1_Load(ByVal sender As System.Object, ByVal e As _
    System.EventArgs) Handles MyBase.Load
    ToolTip1.SetToolTip(Button1, "Open File")
    ToolTip1.SetToolTip(Button2, "Save File")
End Sub
```

There are many more controls like this one, and others, which we won't discuss here. You will discover them as you go.

7.3   Form Events

VSTO has the rich VB.NET *Windows Forms* library behind it, and that library makes VBA's *UserForms* look like dwarfs. What also comes with this new library is a much wider range of events that you can choose from, so you can intercept many more moments than before in the life cycle of *Forms* and its *Controls*. For instance, a *Form* has some 85 different events in VSTO, whereas a *UserForm* had only 22 events. No wonder you have much more control over your *Forms* in VSTO!

Most events carry the following two parameters:

```
Object_Event(ByVal sender As Object, ByVal e As _
    System.Windows.Forms.KeyPressEventArgs) Handles ...
```

> ➤ The variable **sender** refers to the *Object* that called the event. This is only important when one event handler is attached to several Controls.

> ➤ The variable **e** refers to all the event arguments that happen to come with a specific event

In the following example, we will create a *Form* with *Textboxes* and then use their events to validate data entry into the *Form*. This way, we can regulate data entry into the *Worksheet* by channeling data entry through the validation process managed by the *Form*.

1.   The first step is to create the *Form* plus its *Controls*.

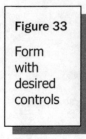

Figure 33

Form with desired controls

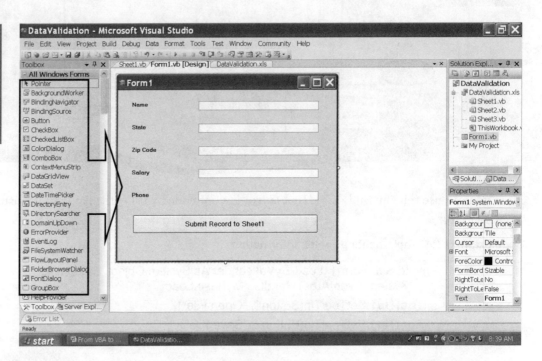

We can use the Form's *Load* event to disable the button until all *Textboxes* have been filled. In order to monitor the user's keystrokes while working in the *Form*, we must set the *Form*'s *KeyPreview* property to *True*. *KeyPreview* is set to *False* by default because there is some overhead to constantly checking keystrokes on the *Form*. But sometimes that's exactly what you want to have happen!

Code Example 25: Checking Keystrokes in a Form

```
Public Class Form1

    Private Sub Form1_Load(ByVal sender As Object, ByVal e As System.EventArgs) _
        Handles Me.Load
        Me.KeyPreview = True
        Me.btnSubmit.Enabled = False
    End Sub

End Class
```

2. Next, we could call the Form from the *StartUp* event of *Sheet1* – preferably in a modal way so the user cannot change the information that has been transferred to the Worksheet.

Code Example 26: Calling a Form from an Event

```
Public Class Sheet1

    Private Sub Sheet1_Startup(ByVal sender As Object, ByVal e As _
        System.EventArgs) Handles Me.Startup
    Dim WF As New Form1
        WF.ShowDialog()
    End Sub

End Class
```

3. Now, we need to enable the button as soon as all *Textboxes* have been filled. A good event to do so is the Form's *KeyUp* event.

Code Example 27: Checking for Empty Textboxes

```
Public Class Form1

    Private Sub Form1_KeyUp(ByVal sender As Object, ByVal e As _
        System.Windows.Forms.KeyEventArgs) Handles Me.KeyUp
    For Each ctl As Control In Me.Controls
        If TypeOf ctl Is TextBox Then
            If CType(ctl, TextBox).Text = "" Then
                Me.btnSubmit.Enabled = False
                Exit Sub
            End If
        End If
    Next
    Me.btnSubmit.Enabled = True
    End Sub

End Class
```

4. We may also want to make sure the user can just hit *Enter* (instead of *Tab*) to move to the next *TextBox*. This could be done from the Form's *KeyDown* event.

Code Example 28: Changing Return Key into Tab Key

```
Public Class Form1

    Private Sub Form1_KeyDown(ByVal sender As Object, ByVal e As _
        System.Windows.Forms.KeyEventArgs) Handles Me.KeyDown
        If e.KeyCode = Keys.Return Then My.Computer.Keyboard.SendKeys("{TAB}")
    End Sub

End Class
```

5. Once the *Submit* button has been enabled, it should transfer all information from the *Form* into *Sheet1*.

Code Example 29: Submitting Form Data to Spreadsheet

```
Public Class Form1

    Private Sub btnSubmit_Click(ByVal sender As Object, ByVal e As _
        System.EventArgs) Handles btnSubmit.Click
        Dim thisWB As Excel.Workbook = CType(Globals.ThisWorkbook, Excel.Workbook)
        Dim AW As Excel.Worksheet = CType(thisWB.ActiveSheet, Excel.Worksheet)
        Dim CR As Excel.Range = AW.Range("A1").CurrentRegion
        With CR
            Dim r As Integer =.Rows.Count
            CR =.Resize(r + 1)
            .Cells(r + 1, 1) = Me.txtName.Text
            .Cells(r + 1, 2) = Me.txtState.Text
            CType(.Cells(r + 1, 3), Excel.Range).NumberFormat = "@"
            .Cells(r + 1, 3) = Me.txtZip.Text
            .Cells(r + 1, 4) = Me.txtSalary.Text
            .Cells(r + 1, 5) = Me.txtPhone.Text
            For Each ctl As Control In Me.Controls
                If TypeOf ctl Is TextBox Then
                    CType(ctl, TextBox).Text = ""
                End If
            Next
            .CurrentRegion.EntireColumn.AutoFit()
        End With
        Me.txtName.Focus()
        Me.btnSubmit.Enabled = False
    End Sub

End Class
```

6. Now it is time to validate information entered into a specific *Textbox*. Let us start with the Textbox *txtName* and make sure that numeric entries in this box will be ignored by using the TextBox' *KeyPress* event.

Code Example 30: Validating TextBoxes for Numeric Entries

```
Public Class Form1

    Private Sub txtName_KeyPress(ByVal sender As Object, ByVal e As _
        System.Windows.Forms.KeyPressEventArgs) Handles txtName.KeyPress
        Select Case e.KeyChar
            Case CChar("0") To CChar("9")
                e.Handled = True
        End Select
    End Sub

End Class
```

7. In *txtState*, we should limit entries to a length of two, and we would like to automatically capitalize its text entry. A proper event to do so would be the *Validating* event; it has a nice *Cancel* option, so the user cannot leave that *Textbox* until emerging problems have been solved.

Code Example 31: Validating TextBoxes for Length of Entries

```
Public Class Form1

    Private Sub txtState_Validating(ByVal sender As Object, ByVal e As _
        System.ComponentModel.CancelEventArgs) Handles txtState.Validating
        If Len(Me.txtState.Text) <> 2 Then
            MsgBox("Two characters please")
            e.Cancel = True
        Else
            txtState.Text = txtState.Text.ToUpper
        End If
    End Sub

End Class
```

8. In *txtZip*, we could do something similar: allowing exactly five numbers — and nothing but numbers!

Code Example 32: Checking TextBoxes for a Certain Amount of Numbers

```
Public Class Form1

    Private Sub txtZip_Validating(ByVal sender As Object, ByVal e As _
        System.ComponentModel.CancelEventArgs) Handles txtZip.Validating
        If IsNumeric(txtZip.Text) = False Then
            MsgBox("Only numbers")
            e.Cancel = True
        ElseIf Len(txtZip.Text) <> 5 Then
            MsgBox("Only 5 numbers")
            e.Cancel = True
        End If
    End Sub

End Class
```

9. When the user exits *txtSalary*, the salary amount should come up in currency format.

Code Example 33: Changing the Format of TextBox Entries

```
Public Class Form1

    Private Sub txtSalary_LostFocus(ByVal sender As Object, ByVal e As _
        System.EventArgs) Handles txtSalary.LostFocus
        If IsNumeric(txtSalary.Text) Then
            Me.txtSalary.Text = CDbl(Me.txtSalary.Text).ToString("$ #,##0.00")
        Else
            Me.txtSalary.Focus()
        End If
    End Sub

End Class
```

10. In *txtPhone*, we will apply some fancy automatic formatting with parentheses and dashes. The *KeyPress* event could take care of the formatting, whereas the *Validating* event checks for the correct length of the phone number.

Code Example 34: Formatting Phone Number Entries in TextBoxes

```
Public Class Form1

    Private Sub txtPhone_KeyPress(ByVal sender As Object, ByVal e As _
        System.Windows.Forms.KeyPressEventArgs) Handles txtPhone.KeyPress
        Select Case e.KeyChar
          Case CChar("0") To CChar("9")
            Dim ch As Char = e.KeyChar
            e.Handled = True
            Select Case Len(Me.txtPhone.Text)
                Case 0 : Me.txtPhone.Text = "(" & ch
                Case 3 : Me.txtPhone.Text = Me.txtPhone.Text & ch & ")-"
                Case 8 : Me.txtPhone.Text = Me.txtPhone.Text & ch & "-"
                Case 14 : MsgBox("The number is complete")
                Case Else : Me.txtPhone.Text = Me.txtPhone.Text & ch
            End Select
          Case Else
            e.Handled = True
        End Select
    End Sub

    Private Sub txtPhone_Validating(ByVal sender As Object, ByVal e As _
        System.ComponentModel.CancelEventArgs) Handles txtPhone.Validating
        If Len(Me.txtPhone.Text) <> 14 Then e.Cancel = True
    End Sub

End Class
```

11. And then, after all of this, be sure to check everything thoroughly before transferring the record to the *Worksheet*.

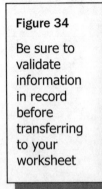

Figure 34

Be sure to validate information in record before transferring to your worksheet

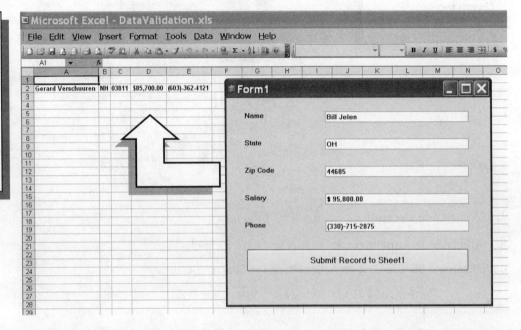

I will leave it up to you to create fancier *Forms* for your applications. I hope you have gained some insights into the *Form* power of VSTO.

7.4   The New ActionsPane

Although the new *ActionsPane* in Office 2003 is not really a form element, it can use form elements – and that's why I will talk about it here. In other words, although an *ActionsPane* is not a real form, you can practically use it as a form on the side. I will limit my discussion at this point to its use for buttons that activate subroutines – thus, the perfect candidates for former VBA macros that have been transferred to VSTO (see 2.5). Later on, we will study another example (see 10.4).

Until things get changed in later VSTO versions, *ActionPanes* have to be implemented by code – for instance, when the *Workbook* starts. The following code creates a *CommandBar* of the *Task Pane* type, uses the *ActionsPane*, and adds a *Label* to the panel – to be followed later by buttons that can make your former macros run.

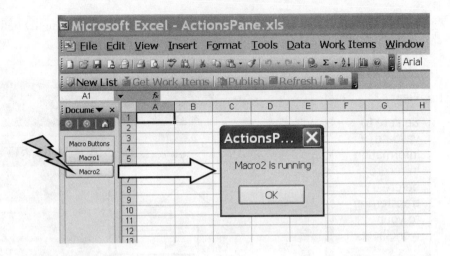

Figure 35

ActionsPane with *CommandBar*

1. Write code to create a *CommandBar* to the left.

2. Add code to implement an *ActionsPane* with a Label.

Code Example 35: Creating an ActionsPane for "Macro" Buttons

```
Public Class ThisWorkbook


    Private Sub ThisWorkbook_Startup(ByVal sender As Object, ByVal e As _
        System.EventArgs) Handles Me.Startup
        Dim CB As Office.CommandBar = Me.Application.CommandBars("Task Pane")
        CB.Width = 100
        CB.Position = Microsoft.Office.Core.MsoBarPosition.msoBarLeft
        Dim lbl As New Label
        lbl.Text = "Macro Buttons"
        lbl.TextAlign = ContentAlignment.MiddleCenter
        Me.ActionsPane.Controls.Add(lbl)
    End Sub

End Class
```

3. The next issue is going to be the buttons. Not only do they need certain property settings, but also an *Event Handler* for when they are clicked.

4. This latter part is done with the keyword *AddHandler*, including a specification as to which event and the keyword *AddressOf*, to indicate which subroutine to run.

5. The *Click* event of each button is going to call *RunMacro*.

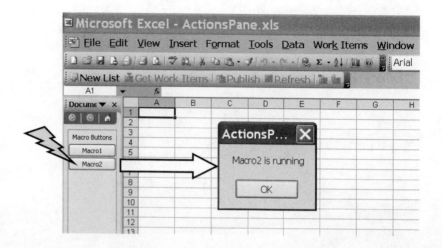

Figure 36

Pressing a Macro button in the *CommandBar* launches a message box indicating the status of the Macro

---

'Add at the end of ThisWorkbook_Startup

Dim btn1 As New Button
btn1.Text = "Macro1"
AddHandler btn1.Click, **AddressOf** RunMacro
Me.ActionsPane.Controls.Add(btn1)
Dim btn2 As New Button
btn2.Text = "Macro2"
AddHandler btn2.Click, **AddressOf** RunMacro
Me.ActionsPane.Controls.Add(btn2)

---

6.   Here is the code for the subroutine *RunMacro* (in a module). Because it runs as an *Event Handler*, you need to include the arguments *sender* and *e*. Thanks to the *sender* argument, we know which button was pressed, so we can decide which macro to run.

Module Module1

```
Sub RunMacro(ByVal sender As Object, ByVal e As System.EventArgs)
    If CType(sender, Button).Text = "Macro1" Then Macro1()
    If CType(sender, Button).Text = "Macro2" Then Macro2()
End Sub

Sub Macro1()
    MsgBox("Macro1 is running")
End Sub

Sub Macro2()
    MsgBox("Macro2 is running")
End Sub

End Module
```

7.5   Case Study: A Rosetta Stone

Figure 37

Clicking on any name in the *ListBox* of
sheet names activates the Worksheet
with that name.

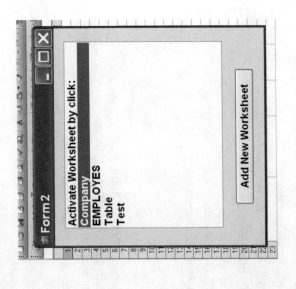

The following code uses a *Form* with two controls: a *Listbox* that gets filled with the names of all worksheets, plus a *Button* that adds a new *Worksheet* to the *Workbook* and then updates the *Listbox*. We leave the sorting up to you.

A click on any name in the *Listbox* activates the *Worksheet* with that name.

An instance of the *Form* gets created and opens automatically when the user opens the *Workbook*, because the code to open the *Form* is located in the *StartUp* event of one of its sheets (say, *Sheet2*).

The *StartUp* event of a sheet kicks in when the *Workbook* opens. The *StartUp* event of a sheet only occurs once in its lifetime, whereas the sheet's *ActivateEvent* may happen repeatedly — and would consequently create several instances of the *Form*'s class.

VBA Version	VSTO Version
	Code Example 36: Displaying Sheet Names in a Form's Listbox
'In UserForm2	Public Class Form2
	Dim **thisWB** As Excel.Workbook = CType(**Globals**.ThisWorkbook, _
	Excel.Workbook)
Private Sub UserForm_Activate()	Private Sub Form2_**Load**(ByVal sender As System.Object, ByVal _
Dim i As Integer	e As System.EventArgs) Handles MyBase.Load
Me.ListBox1.Font.Size = 14	Me.ListBox1.Font = **New Font**("Arial", 14, FontStyle.Bold)
Me.ListBox1.Font.Bold = True	Me.Button1.Font = **New Font**("Arial", 14, FontStyle.Bold)
Me.CommandButton1.Caption = "Insert new sheet"	Me.Button1.Text = "Add New Worksheet"
Me.ListBox1.AddItem "Activate Worksheet by click ."	Me.ListBox1.Items.Add("Activate Worksheet by click:")
For i = 1 To WorkSheets.Count	For i As Integer = 1 To **thisWB**.Worksheets.Count
	Dim **WS** As Excel.Worksheet = _
	CType(**thisWB**.Worksheets(i), Excel.Worksheet)
ListBox1.AddItem WorkSheets(i).Name	Me.ListBox1.Items.Add(**WS**.Name)
Next i	Next
End Sub	End Sub
Private Sub ListBox1_Click()	Private Sub ListBox1_**SelectedIndexChanged**(ByVal sender As _
	Object, ByVal e As System.EventArgs) Handles _
	ListBox1.SelectedIndexChanged
Dim iSel As Integer	Dim i As Integer = Me.ListBox1.**SelectedIndex**
iSel = ListBox1.ListIndex	If i > 0 Then
If iSel > 0 Then WorkSheets(iSel).Select	Dim **WS** As Excel.Worksheet = CType(**thisWB**.Worksheets(i), _
	Excel.Worksheet)
	WS.Select()
	End If
End Sub	End Sub

VBA Version

```
Private Sub CommandButton1_Click()

Dim sht As Worksheet, txt As String, i As Integer
Set sht = Worksheets.Add(, ActiveSheet)
txt = InputBox("Sheet name")
On Error Resume Next

If txt <> "" Then sht.Name = txt
Do Until Err.Number = 0
    Err.Number = 0 ' OR: Err.Clear
    i = i + 1
    sht.Name = txt & i
Loop
Me.ListBox1.Clear
UserForm_Activate

End Sub
```

```
'In Sheet2

Private Sub Worksheet_Activate()

    UserForm2.Show vbModeless
End Sub
```

VSTO Version

```
Private Sub Button1_Click(ByVal sender As Object, ByVal e As _
    System.EventArgs) Handles Button1.Click

Dim sName As String, oSheet As Object
sName = InputBox("Which name?")
If sName = "" Then Exit Sub
If MsgBox("Before current sheet?", MsgBoxStyle.YesNo) = _
        MsgBoxResult.Yes Then
    oSheet = thisWB.Worksheets.Add(thisWB.ActiveSheet)
Else
    oSheet = thisWB.Worksheets.Add(, thisWB.ActiveSheet)
End If
CType(oSheet, Excel.Worksheet).Name = sName
Me.ListBox1.Items.Clear()
Form2_Load(sender, e)

End Sub
End Class
```

```
Public Class Sheet2

Private Sub Sheet2_Startup(ByVal sender As Object, ByVal e _
    As System.EventArgs) Handles Me.Startup

    Dim WF As Form2 = New Form2
    WF.Show()
End Sub

End Class
```

8   Error vs. Exception Handling

8.1   An Improved Alternative

Error handling in VBA has always been primitive – with its *On Error* techniques. One of the reasons for this poor performance is that you cannot install a second error handler in a procedure, because errors from the first handler would be directed to the second one. Another reason is that catching errors in the error handler itself requires hard-to-manage recursive techniques using *On Error GoTo* again. Yet, you can keep applying these older VBA techniques in VSTO, if you choose to do so.

As an alternative, VSTO uses VB.NET's structured *Exception* handling, which means that you can break up code into execution blocks, each of which has its own error handler. The three keywords are *Try*, *Catch*, and *Finally*.

Place the code that might raise an error after the *Try* keyword. Code that does generate an error transfers control to the *Catch* section where the situation can be rectified. Code, however, that executes properly skips the code in the *Catch* section and executes the code in the *Finally* section (if there is any). The *Finally* section will always execute, no matter what happened before; so it is perfect for something like cleanup code, but it is optional.

Table 49	VBA	VSTO
Comparing VBA's Error Handling code with VSTO's Exception handling code	On Error GoTo **errHand**	**Try**
	…	… (protected code)
	Exit Sub	**Catch**
	errHand:	… (correction code)
	Msgbox err.Description	**Finally**
		… (clean-up code)
	'OR use one point of exit instead	**End Try**

Whereas VBA works with the *Err* object, VSTO has several *Exception* classes that handle different groups of exceptions. Consequently, you can have multiple *Catch* statements in one *Try* block, each one handling a different type of error. If you want to query for error information, you need to declare a variable for that specific *Exception* object (without such a variable you cannot access its error information). However, there is also a generic *Exception* class, which you should always place at the end of a series of *Catch* sections, because this one traps everything that wasn't trapped earlier.

```
Try
    …
Catch eFiles As FileNotFoundException
    MsgBox(eFiles.FileName & " wasn't found")
Catch eDivision As DivideByZeroException
    MsgBox(eDivison.Message)
Catch ex As Exception
    MsgBox(ex.Message)
End Try
```

Not only can you have several consecutive *Try* blocks, but also nested blocks. If something goes wrong in the *Finally* section of the inner *Try* block, the outer *Try* block can still trap that problem. So it may be wise to always wrap your code (including exception handlers) inside another *Try* block in order to catch all the remaining problems.

What may make things a bit more complicated in terms of *Exception* handling is the fact that VSTO uses block-level scope for its variables (see 5.3). Consequently, variables declared inside the *Try* block are not visible to other blocks such as *Finally*. Just look at the following example to be discussed later in more detail (see 9.1).

What we need in this example is a second, nested *Try* block in order to make sure that the objects *FS* and *SR* are "visible" to the *Finally* block of the inner *Try* section, where the final cleanup is performed. Without a second *Try* section, *FS* and *SR* would be created in the *Try* block, but would not be "visible" in the *Finally* block (see right panel). The reason is simple but very sound: *FS* and *SR* were declared outside the *Try* block, but they may have failed to be created in the *Try* block, so the *Finally* block may not be able to close what is not there!

Code Example 37: Reading Text Files with Exception Handling

With second *Try* section	Without second *Try* section

Imports System.IO
Module myModule
 	
Sub ReadFromTextFile()
  Try
    Dim FS As FileStream = New FileStream(…)
    Dim SR As StreamReader = New _
      StreamReader(FS)
    Try
      Do
        sLine = SR.ReadLine()
        …
      Loop Until sLine = Nothing
    Catch ex As Exception
      MsgBox(ex.Message)
    Finally
      SR.Close()
      FS.Close()
    End Try
  Catch ex As Exception
    MsgBox(ex.Message)
  End Try
End Sub
	Imports System.IO
	Module myModule
	
	Sub ReadFromTextFile()
	  Try
	    Dim **FS** As FileStream = New FileStream(…)
	    Dim **SR** As StreamReader = New _
	      StreamReader(FS)
	    Do
	      sLine = SR.ReadLine()
	      …
	    Loop Until sLine = Nothing
	  Catch ex As Exception
	    MsgBox(ex.Message)
	  Finally
	    SR.Close()
	    FS.Close()
	  End Try
	End Sub

One more note: Because there is no *Resume* functionality for re-entering the *Try* block, nesting *Try* blocks may be your answer here. A similar story holds for *Resume Next* statements: You have to use a *Try* block instead. By the way, you can still use these older elements of *Error* handling in VSTO as an alternative, but not within the structure of *Exception* handling. So don't try to combine both ways in the same procedure!

Code Example 38: Testing Several Try Configurations

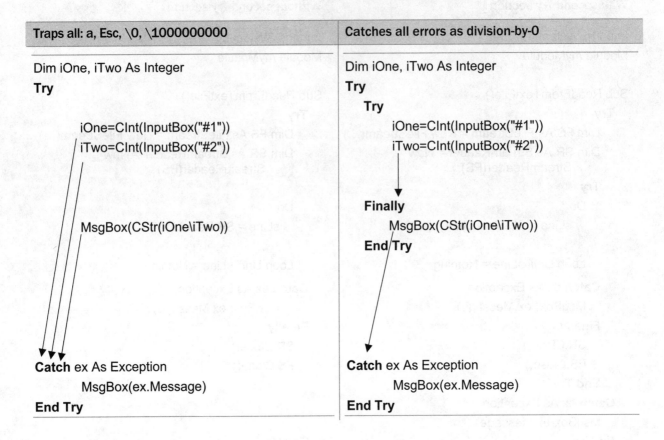

Traps all: a, Esc, \0, \1000000000	Catches all errors as division-by-0

Dim iOne, iTwo As Integer
Try
 	
  iOne=CInt(InputBox("#1"))
  iTwo=CInt(InputBox("#2"))
 	
  MsgBox(CStr(iOne\iTwo))
 	
Catch ex As Exception
  MsgBox(ex.Message)
End Try
	Dim iOne, iTwo As Integer
	Try
	  Try
	    iOne=CInt(InputBox("#1"))
	    iTwo=CInt(InputBox("#2"))
	
	  Finally
	    MsgBox(CStr(iOne\iTwo))
	  End Try
	
	Catch ex As Exception
	  MsgBox(ex.Message)
	End Try

Testing Several Try Configurations, Continued

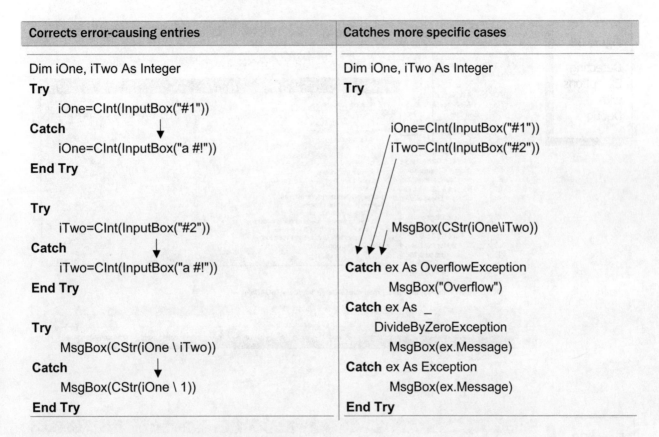

Corrects error-causing entries	Catches more specific cases
| ```
Dim iOne, iTwo As Integer
Try
     iOne=CInt(InputBox("#1"))
Catch
     iOne=CInt(InputBox("a #!"))
End Try

Try
     iTwo=CInt(InputBox("#2"))
Catch
     iTwo=CInt(InputBox("a #!"))
End Try

Try
     MsgBox(CStr(iOne \ iTwo))
Catch
     MsgBox(CStr(iOne \ 1))
End Try
``` | ```
Dim iOne, iTwo As Integer
Try

     iOne=CInt(InputBox("#1"))
     iTwo=CInt(InputBox("#2"))



     MsgBox(CStr(iOne\iTwo))


Catch ex As OverflowException
     MsgBox("Overflow")
Catch ex As _
     DivideByZeroException
     MsgBox(ex.Message)
Catch ex As Exception
     MsgBox(ex.Message)
End Try
``` |

8.2   Some Debugging Issues

Debugging is not directly related to *Error* and *Exception* handling, but I will discuss it in this chapter anyway.

Debugging tools have changed a little after VBA, but I will not go into details here. You will easily discover them on your own when you start working in VSTO. Let me mention, though, that you have more debug windows available. An extremely helpful one is the *Error List*, which logs all errors, including the line at which they occurred. You can either double-click on an error in the list to get to the troubled code line or find the error by its line number (after you number your code lines: *Tools →* *Options → Text Editor → Basic →* ☑ *Line Numbers*).

Another nice feature is the fact that errors get flagged while you are typing your code – much more so than in VBA. Little waves and tooltip texts alert you for missing commas, parentheses, etc., plus they tell you which conversions are illegal.

An interesting issue is that you can select the kinds of exceptions you want to intercept in your debugging sessions: *Debug → Exceptions*. When these exceptions get thrown, you receive a rather detailed report as to what went wrong.

Figure 38

Detecting
Exceptions
with
Debug

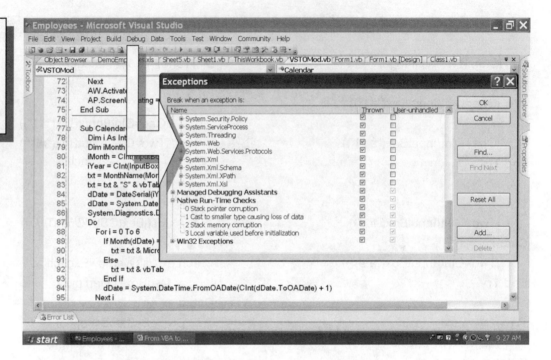

Figure 39

Exceptions
report

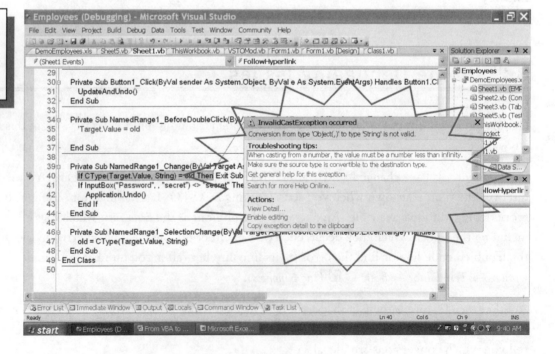

To interrupt and evaluate your code, you will probably still use one of the following tools:

Breakpoints

Set a *breakpoint* to stop your code on the marked line of code before it is executed. When your code encounters a breakpoint, it enters break mode and remains in break mode until you press *F5* to continue execution.

Stop keyword

Use the *Stop* keyword and then open the *Locals Window*, etc.

Watch expressions

Use *Watch* expressions to monitor the value of any variable, property, object, or expression as your code executes. *Watch* expressions also let you specify under which condition your code should enter break mode – for instance, when an expression becomes true or when the value of a variable changes. If you do not have to continually monitor a value, you can use the *Quick Watch* dialog box to quickly check the value of a variable or expression. Just type your variable or expression, and then hit *Enter*.

MessageBoxes

Use *MessageBoxes* – either *MsgBox(...)* or *MessageBox.Show(...)*. These boxes remain helpful tools.

Immediate Window

All *System.Diagnostics.Debug.Write("...")* statements will be output to the *Immediate Window*. When your code is in break mode, the *Immediate Window* has the same scope as the procedure in which the breakpoint is located. This makes it possible for you to test variables (just type *?var* and hit *Enter*) and to change their values (type *var=...*). In addition, you can use this window to call procedures and test them by using different data – without having to run your application from the beginning.

And then we have the famous *step-by-step tool*!

However, the *F8* key from VBA has been replaced with *F11* in VSTO. *F11* does two things. Number 1: If you click inside a procedure, *F11* starts running the entire procedure. Number 2: If you create a breakpoint in code and run the procedure, *F11* makes you go line-by-line from the breakpoint on.

8.3 Case Study: A Rosetta Stone

Figure 40

Selecting a range using an
Input box that can be
cancelled

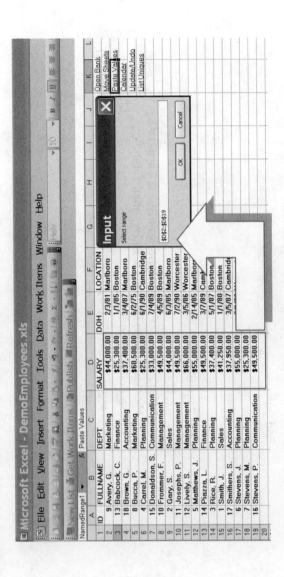

The following code inserts into cell *K3* a *hyperlink* to the custom procedure *PasteValues*.

The procedure *PasteValues* gives users an *Inputbox* that allows them to select the *Range* whose formulas should be changed into values. If the user cancels the *Inputbox*, exception handling kicks in.

Without cancellation, the selected range will be changed from formulas into values. Make sure you test the code on a protected sheet so the outer *Try* section kicks in.

VBA Version	VSTO Version

Code Example 39: Using InputBoxes with Exception Handling

'Call the macro with a shortcut, or ...

```
Public Class ThisWorkbook

Private Sub ThisWorkbook_Open() Handles Me.Open
    Dim WS As Excel.Worksheet = _
        CType(ThisApplication.Sheets(1), Excel.Worksheet)
    WS.Activate()
    Dim HL As Excel.Hyperlink
    HL = CType(WS.Hyperlinks.Add(WS.Range("K3"), "", , , _
        "Paste Values"), Excel.Hyperlink)

End Sub

End Class

Public Class Sheet1

Private Sub Sheet1_FollowHyperlink(ByVal Target As _
    Microsoft.Office.Interop.Excel.Hyperlink) Handles _
    Me.FollowHyperlink
    If Target.TextToDisplay = "Paste Values" Then PastingValues()
End Sub

End Class
```

VBA Version	VSTO Version
| ```
'In Module

Sub PastingValues()
On Error GoTo errTrap

Dim myRange As Range
Set myRange = ActiveSheet.Selection

Set myRange = Application.InputBox("Select range", , , , , 8)

myRange.Copy
myRange.PasteSpecial xlPasteValues
Application.CutCopyMode = False
Exit Sub
errTrap:
    MsgBox("You decided to cancel")

End Sub
``` | ```
Module myModule

Dim thisWB As Excel.Workbook = CType(Globals.ThisWorkbook, _
    Excel.Workbook)

Sub PastingValues()
Dim WS As Excel.Worksheet = CType(thisWB.ActiveSheet, _
    Excel.Worksheet)

Dim myRange As Excel.Range = _
    CType(WS.Application.Selection, Excel.Range)

Try
    Try
        myRange = CType(thisWB.Application.InputBox("Select" & _
            " range", , , , , 8), Excel.Range)

    Catch
        MsgBox("You decided to cancel")
    End Try
    myRange.Copy()
    myRange.PasteSpecial(Excel.XlPasteType.xlPasteValues)
    thisWB.Application.CutCopyMode = CType(False, _
        Excel.XlCutCopyMode)

    Catch ex As Exception
        MsgBox(ex.Message)
    End Try
End Sub

End Module
``` |

Figure 41

General error code causes
error message box to display

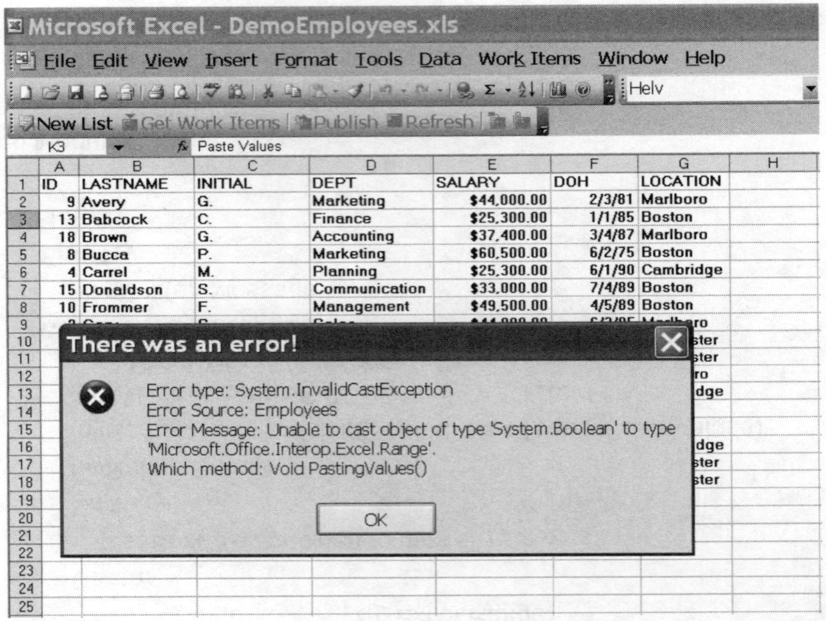

The following code creates a general error handler — called *ErrorAlert()*
— that can be applied to almost any error situation. It passes the
Exception object through a parameter: *ErrorAlert(ex As Exception)*

The subroutine is placed in a general *Module*; it informs the user about
the error and takes appropriate action to reset all kinds of general
settings for the system.

You can call this method from several procedures. It is too general,
though, for more specific exception checking.

I actually called this new method in the subroutine *PasteValues()*, which I
discussed in the previous case study. When the user cancels this
inputbox, the *ErrorAlert()* method kicks in, including an extensive
error/exception message.

Tip:

*Make sure you have turned internal Exception alerts OFF: Debug →
Exceptions. Otherwise those alerts will kick in first.*

Code Example 40: Creating General Exception Handlers

VBA Version	VSTO Version

VBA Version

```
'In Module

Sub ErrAlert()
    MsgBox "Error number: " & Err.Number & vbCr & _
        "Description: " & Err.Description & vbCr & _
        "Source: " & Err.Source & vbCr & _
        "There was an error", Err.HelpFile, Err.HelpContext

    Application.ScreenUpdating = True
    Application.DisplayAlerts = True
    Application.Interactive = True
    Application.Cursor = xlDefault
End Sub


Sub AnyMethod()
    On Error GoTo errTrap
    ...
    Exit Sub
errTrap:
    ErrAlert
End Sub
```

VSTO Version

```
Module myModule
    Dim thisWB As Excel.Workbook = _
        CType(Globals.ThisWorkbook, Excel.Workbook)

    Sub ErrorAlert(ByVal ex As Exception)
        MsgBox("Error type: " & ex.GetType().ToString & vbCr & _
            "Error Source: " & ex.Source & vbCr & _
            "Error Message: " & ex.Message & vbCr & _
            "Which method: " & ex.TargetSite.ToString, _
            MsgBoxStyle.Critical, "There was an error!")

        thisWB.Application.ScreenUpdating = True
        thisWB.Application.DisplayAlerts = True
        thisWB.Application.Interactive = True
        thisWB.Application.Cursor = Excel.XlMousePointer.xlDefault
    End Sub

End Module


Sub anyMethod()
    Try
        ...
    Catch ex As Exception
        ErrorAlert(ex)
    End Try
End Sub
```

9 File Management

9.1 Text Files

In VBA, it was possible to write data to *.txt* or *.bin* files by using statements such as this one: *Open sFile For Output As iFile*. And then you could do something similar to read them back into Excel. Thanks to VB.NET, VSTO offers a more "streamlined" system. Classes that make all of this possible can be found in the namespace *System.IO*.

After importing this namespace, you can read and write from a stream by using a *StreamReader()* or *StreamWriter()* object created from their respective classes. In this chapter, we will just focus on *Text* streams (although there is also a *BinaryWriter()* and *BinaryReader()* Class for binary data; see 9.2).

The *StreamReader* and *StreamWriter* object work either with a file name string or with a so-called *FileStream* object. The *FileStream()* object is a perfect channel between your application and the file, because the *FileStream* class provides random access to a disk file and allows you to specify whether you want to create or open a file, and how to do so.

	Write to File	Read from File
Table 50 Comparing VSTO's StreamWriter and StreamReader code	Imports **System.IO**	
	Dim FS As New **FileStream**(path, filemode)	
	Dim SW As New **StreamWriter**(FS)	Dim SR As New **StreamReader**(FS)
	SW.**Write**("…")	str = SR.**ReadToEnd**()

	For i = 0 To arr.Length-1
	    SW.**WriteLine**(CStr(arr(i)))
	Next
		Do
		    str = SR.**ReadLine**()
		Loop Until str(0) = Nothing

	For Each cell in .CurrentRegion
	    SW.**WriteLine**(CStr(cell))
	Next
		Do While SR.Peek <> -1
		    str = SR.**ReadLine**()
		Loop

	SW.Close() FS.Close()	SR.Close() FS.Close()

Because file manipulation is prone to errors, you should certainly consider *Exception* handlers here. However, you must remain aware of the fact that the *Try/Catch/Finally* structure uses block-level scope (see 5.3 and 8.1), so variables declared in one block are not "visible" in another block. In order to get around this problem, you have at least two options:

1. Separate the object's declaration from the object's creation.

2. Use a second, nested *Try* block inside the first *Try* block.

The first option would look like the solution in the left panel below. The panel to the right is not possible because the objects *FS* and *SR* are created in the *Try* block and are therefore not "visible" after the *End Try* block, when we want to close objects that we may have opened in vain. A solution would be to place the closing actions inside a *Finally* block, but whatever is declared and created in a *Try* block is again not "visible" to the *Finally* block. That's where the second option comes in as a viable alternative.

Code Example 41: Writing and Reading Text Files with Exception Handling

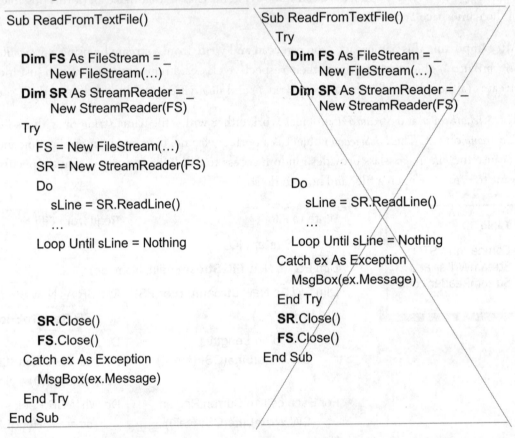

```
Sub ReadFromTextFile()

    Dim FS As FileStream = _
        New FileStream(…)
    Dim SR As StreamReader = _
        New StreamReader(FS)
    Try
        FS = New FileStream(…)
        SR = New StreamReader(FS)
        Do
            sLine = SR.ReadLine()
            …
        Loop Until sLine = Nothing



        SR.Close()
        FS.Close()
    Catch ex As Exception
        MsgBox(ex.Message)
    End Try
End Sub
```

```
Sub ReadFromTextFile()
    Try
        Dim FS As FileStream = _
            New FileStream(…)
        Dim SR As StreamReader = _
            New StreamReader(FS)


        Do
            sLine = SR.ReadLine()
            …
        Loop Until sLine = Nothing
    Catch ex As Exception
        MsgBox(ex.Message)
    End Try
    SR.Close()
    FS.Close()
End Sub
```

If you want to make sure that the closing actions at the end will be done even after trouble, you need a *Finally* block. But again, you need to consider here the block-level scope issue by using the second option: a *Try* block inside a *Try* block – otherwise the objects *FS* and *FR* created in the *Try* block are not "visible" for the *Finally* block.

Code Example 42: Using FileStreams with Nested Try Blocks

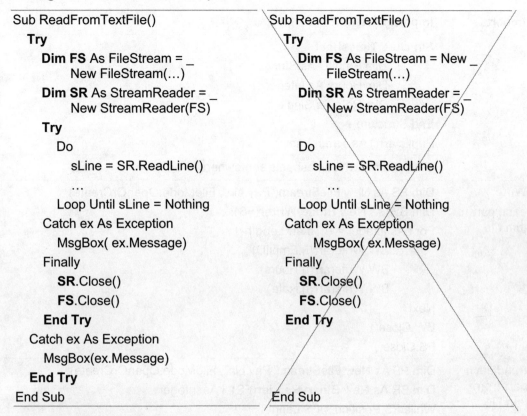

```
Sub ReadFromTextFile()
  Try
    Dim FS As FileStream = _
      New FileStream(…)
    Dim SR As StreamReader = _
      New StreamReader(FS)
    Try
      Do
        sLine = SR.ReadLine()
        …
      Loop Until sLine = Nothing
    Catch ex As Exception
      MsgBox( ex.Message)
    Finally
      SR.Close()
      FS.Close()
    End Try
  Catch ex As Exception
    MsgBox(ex.Message)
  End Try
End Sub
```

```
Sub ReadFromTextFile()
  Try
    Dim FS As FileStream = New _
      FileStream(…)
    Dim SR As StreamReader = _
      New StreamReader(FS)
      Do
        sLine = SR.ReadLine()
        …
      Loop Until sLine = Nothing
    Catch ex As Exception
      MsgBox( ex.Message)
    Finally
      SR.Close()
      FS.Close()
    End Try
End Sub
```

I must admit things used to be easier in VBA where we had that loose statement *On Error Resume Next* - unless you still want to use these older and simpler statements in VSTO as well. We report, you decide.

9.2   Binary Files

When would you use *Binary* streams? First of all, you need them for all non-readable entities such as pictures. But you can also use them for listings based on *Structures* (*Structure* is VSTO's keyword for custom *Types*; see 6.2). You can write *Structures* (including arrays of *Structures*) to *.bin* files and then read them back again.

Code Example 43: Writing Structures to Binary Files

Imports	Imports System.IO

	Structure **Timesheet**
	        Dim EmplID As String
	        Dim Hours As Integer
	        Dim Rate As Single
	End Structure
	Public **arr**() As **Timesheet**

	'Fill the array with timesheets somewhere

Write each part to .bin file	Dim FS As New FileStream("Pay.bin", FileMode.OpenOrCreate)
	Dim BW As New **BinaryWriter**(FS)
	For i As Integer = 0 To arr.Length-1
	        BW.Write(**arr**(i).EmplID)
	        BW.Write(**arr**(i).Hours)
	        BW.Write(**arr**(i).Rate)
	Next
	BW.Close()
	FS.Close()

Read each part from .bin file	Dim FS As New FileStream("Pay.bin", FileMode.OpenOrCreate)
	Dim BR As New **BinaryReader**(FS), i As Integer
	While FS.Position < FS.Length
	        arr(i).EmplID = BR.ReadString
	        arr(i).Hours = BR.ReadInteger
	        arr(i).Rate) = BR.ReadSingle
	        i += 1
	End While
	BR.Close()
	FS.Close()

Obviously, you could also have stored this structured array in a simple *Text* file – which would take us back to the *StreamReader()* and *StreamWriter()* of 9.1. So the method we used here is kind of clumsy, because you have to control each part of the structure individually. It would be better to treat each *Structure* – or even the total array of *Structures* – as a comprehensive unit so that you can read and write it as a single unit. This can be done by using the *BinaryFormatter()* class located in the namespace *System.Runtime.Serialization.Formatters.Binary*.

The *BinaryFormatter()* class allows you to handle arrays, *ArrayLists*, *Structures*, etc., as one comprehensive entity. However, you have to make sure you are dealing with entities that have been declared *Serializable*. Let's use the previous example again, but this time we will store each *Structure* in an *ArrayList* so we can write the *ArrayList* to a *.bin* file as one single unit (and then read the information back into the *ArrayList*).

Code Example 44: Writing an ArrayList of Structures to Binary File

Imports	Imports System.IO **Imports System.Runtime.Serialization.Formatters.Binary**

	<Serializable> Structure **Timesheet**
	      Dim EmplID As String
	      Dim Hours As Integer
	      Dim Rate As Single
	End Structure
	Public **arr** As **New ArrayList**

Fill List	Dim **temp** As New **Timesheet** temp.EmplID = "Trudy" temp.Hours = 40 temp.Rate = 18.95 **arr**.Add(**temp**)

Write array to .bin file	Dim FS As New FileStream("c:\Pay.bin", FileMode.OpenOrCreate, FileAccess.Write)
	Dim BF As New **BinaryFormatter**
	Try
	    BF.**Serialize**(FS, **arr**)
	Catch ex As Exception
	    MsgBox(ex.Message)
	Finally
	    FS.Close()
	End Try

Read array from .bin file	Dim FS As New FileStream("c:\Pay.bin", FileMode.OpenOrCreate, FileAccess.Read)
	Dim BF As New **BinaryFormatter**
	Try
	    arr = CType(BF.**Deserialize**(FS), ArrayList)
	Catch ex As Exception
	    MsgBox(ex.Message)
	Finally
	    FS.Close()
	End Try

Show results	For i As Integer = 0 To arr.Count - 1
	    MsgBox(CType(**arr**(i), Timesheet).EmplID)
	    MsgBox(CType(**arr**(i), Timesheet).Hours)
	    MsgBox(CType(**arr**(i), Timesheet).Rate)
	Next

9.3   Dialog Controls for File Management

Although the *Application* class still provides methods such as *GetOpenFileName()* and *GetSaveAsFileName()* – left over from the good old VBA times – you may want to try some powerful new controls that you can find on the *Toolbox* in the *Dialogs* section. Each option here represents a class; by dragging one of these controls onto the *Form,* you create an instance of that specific class. Each instance will appear at the bottom of the screen, so you can use its properties and methods for your file management.

If you do not rename the objects that were created from these classes, they will probably show up as *ColorDialog1*, *FontDialog1*, *OpenFileDialog1*, *SaveFileDialog1*, etc.

Figure 42

Dragging "invisible" dialog controls onto a *Form*

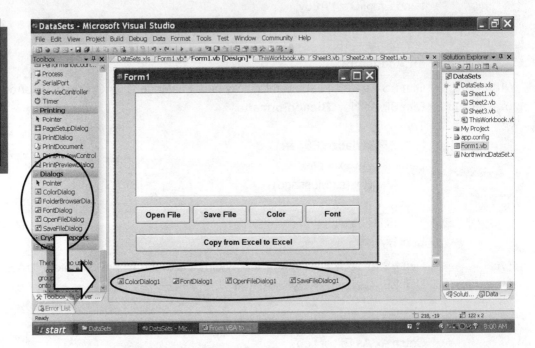

Now you can use these "invisible" controls at the bottom (including their properties and methods) according to your needs. In this case, I placed a few buttons under a *RichTextBox* control. With these buttons, you can open and close files, plus change the color and font of the text as displayed in the *RichTextBox*.

1. The first button opens *.txt* and *.rtf* files. Make sure you separate filter items with the vertical slash symbol, "|", (found above the backward slash key: *Shift*+\).

Code Example 45: Using the OpenFileDialog Control

```
Private Sub Button1_Click(ByVal sender As System.Object, ByVal e As _
    System.EventArgs) Handles Button1.Click
    Try
        Me.OpenFileDialog1.Filter = "RTF Files|*.rtf|Text Files|*.txt"
        Me.OpenFileDialog1.InitialDirectory = Globals.ThisWorkbook.Path
        If Me.OpenFileDialog1.ShowDialog = Windows.Forms.DialogResult.OK Then
            Me.RichTextBox1.LoadFile(Me.OpenFileDialog1.FileName)
        End If
    Catch ex As Exception
        MessageBox.Show(ex.Message)
    End Try
End Sub
```

2. The second buttons saves files by default as *.rtf*.

Code Example 46: Using the SaveFileDialog Control

```
Private Sub Button2_Click(ByVal sender As Object, ByVal e As _
    System.EventArgs) Handles Button2.Click
    Try
        Me.SaveFileDialog1.Filter = "RTF Files|*.rtf|Text Files|*.txt"
        Me.SaveFileDialog1.DefaultExt = "rtf"
        If Me.SaveFileDialog1.ShowDialog = Windows.Forms.DialogResult.OK Then
            Me.RichTextBox1.SaveFile(Me.SaveFileDialog1.FileName)
        End If
    Catch ex As Exception
        MessageBox.Show(ex.Message)
    End Try
End Sub
```

3. The third button changes the font color in the *RichTextBox*, unless the user cancels the *Dialog* box.

Code Example 47: Using the ColorDialog Control

```
Private Sub Button3_Click(ByVal sender As Object, ByVal e As _
    System.EventArgs) Handles Button3.Click
    Me.ColorDialog1.Color = Me.RichTextBox1.ForeColor
    If Me.ColorDialog1.ShowDialog = Windows.Forms.DialogResult.OK Then
        Me.RichTextBox1.ForeColor = Me.ColorDialog1.Color
    End If
End Sub
```

4. The fourth button does something similar: It changes the font settings for the *RichTextBox*.

Code Example 48: Using the FontDialog Control

```
Private Sub Button4_Click(ByVal sender As Object, ByVal e As _
    System.EventArgs) Handles Button4.Click
    Me.FontDialog1.Font = Me.RichTextBox1.Font
    If Me.FontDialog1.ShowDialog = Windows.Forms.DialogResult.OK Then
        Me.RichTextBox1.Font = Me.FontDialog1.Font
    End If
End Sub
```

5. The fifth button copies cell ranges between *.xls* files and lets the user choose what to copy and where to paste. This time, I didn't use a *Dialog* control, but rather the *FileDialog* property of the *Application* as an alternative. The *FileDialog* property offers many great methods, including the *Show*() method, which returns 0 if canceled. In addition, I stored the values of a range as an *Object* type, which can also hold arrays (see 6.3).

Code Example 49: Using the Application's FileDialog Property

```
Private Sub Button5_Click(ByVal sender As System.Object, ByVal e As _
    System.EventArgs) Handles Button5.Click
    Dim thisWB As Excel.Workbook = CType(Globals.ThisWorkbook, Excel.Workbook)
    Dim AW As Excel.Worksheet = CType(thisWB.ActiveSheet, Excel.Worksheet)
    Dim myCopyRange As Excel.Range = _
        CType(thisWB.Application.InputBox ("Select Range", , , , , , , 8), Excel.Range)
    Dim r As Integer = myCopyRange.Rows.Count
    Dim c As Integer = myCopyRange.Columns.Count
    Dim myRangeCopy As Object = CType(myCopyRange.Value2, Object)
    With Globals.ThisWorkbook.ThisApplication.FileDialog _
        (Microsoft.Office.Core.MsoFileDialogType.msoFileDialogOpen)
        .AllowMultiSelect = False
        .Filters.Clear()
        .Filters.Add("Excel Files", "*.xls")
        If .Show <> 0 Then .Execute()
    End With
    AW = CType(Globals.ThisWorkbook.ActiveSheet, Excel.Worksheet)
    Dim myPasteRange As Excel.Range = _
        CType(AW.Application.InputBox( "Where to paste", , , , , , , 8), Excel.Range)
    myPasteRange = myPasteRange.Resize(r, c)
    myPasteRange.Value2 = CType(myRangeCopy, System.Array)
End Sub
```

9.4   Case Study: A Rosetta Stone

Figure 43

Exporting a range of cells to a text file

	A	B	C	D	E	F	G	H
1	ID	LASTNAME	INITIAL	DEPT	SALARY	DOH	LOCATION	
2	9	Avery	G.	Marketing	$44,000.00	2/3/81	Marlboro	
3	13	Babcock	C.	Finance	$25,300.00	1/1/85	Boston	
4	18	Brown	G.	Accounting	$37,400.00	3/4/87	Marlboro	
5	8	Bucca	P.	Marketing	$60,500.00	6/2/75	Boston	
6	4	Carrel	M.	Planning	$25,300.00	6/1/90	Cambridge	
7	15	Donaldson	S.	Communication	$33,000.00	7/4/89	Boston	
8	10	Frommer	F.	Management	$49,500.00	4/5/89	Boston	
9	2	Gary	S.	Sales	$44,000.00	6/3/85	Marlboro	
10	11	Josephs	P.	Management	$49,500.00	7/2/90	Worcester	
11	12	Lively	S.	Management	$66,000.00	3/5/86	Worcester	
12	5	Matthews	J.	Planning	$55,000.00	2/14/85	Marlboro	
13	14	Piazza	L.	Finance	$49,500.00	3/7/89	Cambridge	
14	3	Rice	R.	Planning	$37,400.00	5/1/87	Boston	
15	1	Smith	J.	Sales	$41,250.00	1/1/80	Boston	
16	17	Smithers	S.	Accounting	$37,950.00	3/5/87	Cambridge	
17	6	Stevens	J.	Planning	$55,000.00	8/1/90	Worcester	
18	7	Stevens	M.	Planning	$25,300.00	3/5/90	Worcester	
19	16	Stevens	P.	Communication	$49,500.00	3/5/90	Boston	
20								
21								

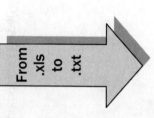

From
.xls
to
.txt

The following code is capable of exporting any range of cells into a text file by using *comma-space* as a delimiter.

The text file will be saved as *Export.txt* and stored in the same folder as *ThisWorkbook*. I did add code to offer users the option of an alternative file name.

The code also asks the user which range to export. The code is lengthy at this point because the user may want to start on another sheet.

The code also uses exception handling in case something goes wrong during the exporting procedure.

Needless to say, we can use the *FileStream()* and *StreamWriter()* classes only after importing the *System.IO* namespace (otherwise we would need much longer addresses).

VBA Version	VSTO Version

Code Example 50: Creating Text Files with the StreamWriter Class

VSTO Version

```
Option Strict On
Imports System.IO

Module myModule

Dim thisWB As Excel.Workbook = CType(Globals.ThisWorkbook, _
   Excel.Workbook)

Sub WriteToTextFile()
Try
   Dim sPath As String = thisWB.Path & "\" & _
      InputBox("File name?", , "Export.txt")
   Dim FS As FileStream= New FileStream(sPath, _
      FileMode.OpenOrCreate)
   Dim SW As StreamWriter = New StreamWriter(FS)
   Try
      Dim sInput As String = InputBox("Start" & _
         "at this sheet: A1 OR: Sheet1!A1)", , "A1")
      Dim AW As Excel.Worksheet = _
         CType(thisWB.ActiveSheet, Excel.Worksheet)
      If InStr(sInput, "!") > 0 Then
         Dim sWS As String = Left(sInput, InStr(sInput, "!") - 1)
         sInput = Right(sInput, Len(sInput) - Len(sWS) - 1)

         AW = CType(thisWB.Worksheets(sWS), Excel.Worksheet)
         AW.Select()
      End If
```

VBA Version

```
'In Module

Sub WriteToTextFile()
On Error GoTo errTrap
Dim sPath As String, sInput As String, sWS As String, CR As _
   Range
sPath = ActiveWorkbook.Path & "\" & _
   InputBox("File name?", , "Export.txt")

sInput = InputBox("Start at this sheet: A1 OR: Sheet1!A1)", , "A1")

If InStr(sInput, "!") > 0 Then
   sWS = Left(sInput, InStr(sInput, "!") - 1)
   sInput = Right(sInput, Len(sInput) - Len(sWS) - 1)

   Set AW = Worksheets(sWS)
   AW.Select
End If
```

VBA Version

```
Set CR = ActiveSheet.Range(sInput).CurrentRegion
For i = 1 To CR.Rows.Count
    sLine = ""
    For j = 1 To CR.Columns.Count
        sLine = sLine & CR.Cells(i, j) & " , "

    Next

Next


    Close iFile


Exit Sub
errTrap:
    MsgBox "Error: " & Err.Description
End Sub
```

VSTO Version

```
Dim CR As Excel.Range = AW.Range(sInput).CurrentRegion
For i As Integer = 1 To CR.Rows.Count
    Dim sLine As String = ""
    For j As Integer = 1 To CR.Columns.Count
        sLine = sLine & CStr(CType(CR.Cells(i, j), _
            Excel.Range).Value) & " , "

    Next
        SW.WriteLine(sLine)

    Next
    Catch ex As Exception
        MsgBox("There was a problem: " & ex.Message)
    Finally
        SW.Close()
        FS.Close()
    End Try
    Catch ex As Exception
        Msgbox(ex.Message)
    End Try
End Sub

End Module
```

Figure 44

Importing a text file into cells in a *Worksheet*

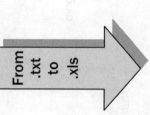

From
.txt
to
.xls

The following code is capable of importing any text file into Excel by calling a *Dialog* box for opening text files – by way of the method *GetOpenFileName()*.

We assume that the text file has *comma-space* as a delimiter, so each text line is cut into pieces (stored into an array of strings) by using the *Split()* method for the delimiter *comma-space*.

Then the array is used to start filling cells on a new *Worksheet* – text line after text line until there are no lines left.

The code uses exception handling again in case something goes wrong during the importing process.

Code Example 51: Reading Text Files with GetOpenFileName and StreamReader

VBA Version

```
'In Module

Sub ReadFromTextFile()
  On Error Resume Next
  Dim sFile As String, iFile As Integer
  Dim sText As String, i As Long, j As Integer
  Dim arr() As Variant, subArr As Variant, WS As Worksheet

  iFile = FreeFile
  sFile = Application.GetOpenFilename("Text, *.txt")
  If sFile = "False" Then Exit Sub
  Open sFile For Input As iFile
  Do Until EOF(iFile)
    ReDim Preserve arr(i)
    Line Input #iFile, arr(i)
    i = i + 1
  Loop
  Close iFile
  For i = 0 To UBound(arr)
    subArr = Split(arr(i), ",")
```

VSTO Version

```
Option Strict On
Imports System.IO

Module myModule

Dim thisWB As Excel.Workbook = CType(Globals.ThisWorkbook, _
  Excel.Workbook)

Sub ReadFromTextFile()
  Try
    Dim sPath As String = _
      CStr(thisWB.Application.GetOpenFilename("Text, *.txt"))
    Dim FS As FileStream = New FileStream(sPath, _
      FileMode.Open)
    Dim SR As StreamReader = New StreamReader(FS)
    Dim sLine As String, n As Integer, arr() As String
    Try
      Dim AW As Excel.Worksheet = _
        CType(thisWB.Worksheets.Add(), Excel.Worksheet)
      Do
        sLine = SR.ReadLine()
        arr = Split(sLine, ",")
        n += 1
        For i As Integer = 1 To arr.Length
          AW.Range("A1").Cells(n, i) = arr(i - 1)
        Next
      Loop Until sLine = Nothing
```

From VBA to VSTO: Is Excel's New Engine for You?

VBA Version

```
    arr(i) = subArr
Next i
Set WS = Worksheets.Add()
For i = 0 To UBound(arr)
  For j = 0 To UBound(arr(i))
    WS.Cells(i+1, j+1) = arr(i)(j)    OR: WS.Cells(1,1).Offset(i, j) = …
  Next j
Next i
WS.Cells().EntireColumn.AutoFit
End Sub
```

VSTO Version

```
        AW.Cells().EntireColumn.AutoFit()
    Catch ex As Exception
        MsgBox(ex.Message)
    Finally
        SR.Close()
        FS.Close()
    End Try
  Catch ex As Exception
      MsgBox(ex.Message)
  End Try
End Sub

End Module
```

10   External Databases

By external databases I mean *Access* databases as well as databases residing on *SQL* or *Oracle* servers. VSTO has three different libraries to deal with these kinds of databases:

There is still the *DAO library*, especially a good fit for local Access databases; I will discuss this library soon, but very briefly. DAO stands for *Data Access Objects*.

Then there is the *ADO library*, probably well-known to most VBA users. This library is useful for any kind of database, including *SQL* and *Oracle Server* databases. ADO stands for *ActiveX Data Objects*.

And finally, we have gained access to the crown jewel of database management: the *ADO.NET library* – and that's where VSTO differs significantly from VBA.

Let us discuss each library in greater detail, so you can (still) use them in VSTO or decide what your favorite one is going to be. I'll bet it's going to be #3: ADO.NET.

10.1 DAO Library

Many developers have some kind of disdain for this "old" system of database management. However, don't sell it short too soon. If you work mainly or only with local Access databases, the DAO library offers you faster performance than ADO – because DAO was specifically designed for this purpose.

Let's say that you just want to load records from an Access database into a new Excel Worksheet. The code you would use in VSTO is practically identical to the code you would have used in VBA. The only differences would be the following:

➢ No Set keywords anymore, of course

➢ Worksheet references have become a little more convoluted

➢ Remember to add a new *Reference* to the latest DAO library:
   Project → Add Reference → COM tab (!) *→ MS DAO Object Library*

Let's assume that your target is the *Suppliers* table in the *Northwind.mdb* database and that you want to display all its records on a new sheet whenever the user activates *Sheet3*. The following code would do so using the DAO library – after setting a *Reference*. If you also use *Imports dao*, you can use *Recordset* instead of *dao.Recordset*, etc. Be prepared for the possibility that you may have to change the location for the *.mdb* file on your machine.

Code Example 52: Importing Database Records with DAO into Spreadsheet

```
Imports dao 'After adding its Reference

Public Class Sheet1

    Private Sub Sheet1_Startup(ByVal sender As Object, ByVal e As System.EventArgs) _
        Handles Me.Startup
        Dim DE As DBEngine, DB As Database, RS As Recordset
        DE = New DBEngine
        DB = DE.OpenDatabase("C:\Program Files\" & _
            "Microsoft Office\OFFICE11\SAMPLES\Northwind.mdb")
        RS = DB.OpenRecordset("Suppliers")
        Dim WS As Excel.Worksheet = CType(Me.Application.Worksheets.Add, _
            Excel.Worksheet)
        For i As Integer = 0 To RS.Fields.Count - 1
            WS.Cells(1, i + 1) = RS.Fields(i).Name
            CType(WS.Cells(1, i + 1), Excel.Range).Interior.ColorIndex = 15
        Next i
        WS.Range("A2").CopyFromRecordset(RS)
        WS.Columns.AutoFit()
        WS.Rows.AutoFit()
    End Sub

End Class
```

Figure 45   Importing database records with DAO into a *spreadsheet* by using code from Example 52

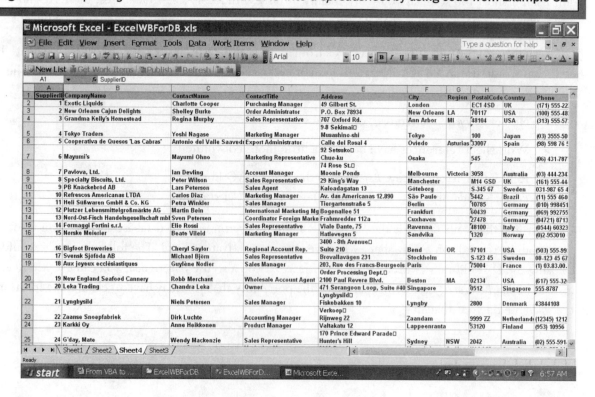

10.2 ADO Library

If you are rather familiar with the ADO library in VBA, you may decide to stay with the original ADO version as you migrate to VSTO. If so, you probably want to know which adjustments you need to make in VSTO. Most ADO classes are still the same – such as *ADODB.Connection*, *ADODB.Recordset*, and *ADODB.Command*.

Say you had created a *UserForm* in VBA that contains a *ListBox* displaying all Company Names of the *Suppliers* table stored in the database *Northwind.mdb*. A click on any name in the *ListBox* provides detailed information about that specific company in *Textboxes*, where you can correct individual records and/or add new records.

Unfortunately, you must create a new *Form* in VSTO (see 13.2), but the code itself would not be much different from what you would have had in VBA. After creating a new *Form* and adding a *Reference* to the latest *Microsoft ActiveX Data Objects Library* (e.g. 2.8), you could use your existing VBA code with some minor VSTO adjustments (mainly explicit conversions).

Figure 46

Importing database records with DAO into a *Form*

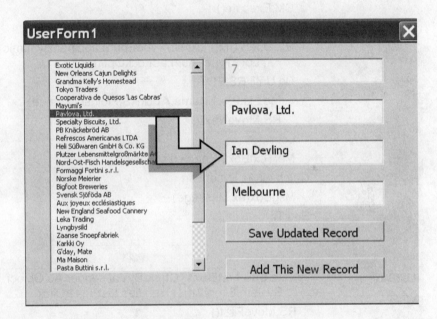

Code Example 53: Importing Database Records with ADO into a Form

```
Public Class ThisWorkbook

    Private Sub ThisWorkbook_Startup(ByVal sender As Object, ByVal e As _
        System.EventArgs) Handles Me.Startup
        Dim WF As New Form1
        WF.Show()
    End Sub

End Class
```

Top of the Form	**Imports ADODB** 'After adding a Reference to the Data Objects library
	    '(located under the COM tab!).
	
	Public Class Form1
	    Dim CN As New **Connection**
	    Dim CM As New **Command**
	    Dim RS As New **Recordset**

Form Load	Private Sub **Form1_Load**(ByVal sender As System.Object, ByVal e As _
	    System.EventArgs) Handles MyBase.Load
	Try
	  CN.ConnectionString = "Provider=Microsoft.Jet.OLEDB.4.0;Data Source=" & _
	    "'C:\Program Files\Microsoft Office\OFFICE11\SAMPLES\Northwind.mdb'"
	  CN.Open()
	  CM.ActiveConnection = CN
	  CM.CommandType = CommandTypeEnum.adCmdText
	  CM.CommandText = "SELECT * From Suppliers"
	  CM.Execute()
	  RS.ActiveConnection = CN
	  RS.Open(CM, , CursorTypeEnum.adOpenDynamic _
	    , LockTypeEnum.adLockOptimistic)
	  Do Until RS.EOF
	    Me.ListBox1.**Items.Add**(RS.Fields(1).Value)
	    RS.**MoveNext**()
	  Loop
	  Me.TextBox1.Enabled = False
	Catch ex As Exception
	  MsgBox(ex.Message)
	End Try
	End Sub

ListBox Click	Private **Sub ListBox1_Click**(ByVal sender As Object, ByVal e As _
	    System.EventArgs) Handles ListBox1.Click
	  RS.MoveFirst()
	  RS.Move(Me.ListBox1.**SelectedIndex**)
	  Me.TextBox1.Text = CStr(RS.Fields(0).Value)
	  Me.TextBox2.Text = CStr(RS.Fields(1).Value)
	  Me.TextBox3.Text = CStr(RS.Fields(2).Value)
	  Me.TextBox4.Text = CStr(RS.Fields(5).Value)
	End Sub

| **Button1 Click** | ```
Private Sub Button1_Click(ByVal sender As Object, ByVal e As _
     System.EventArgs) Handles Button1.Click
    RS.Fields(1).Value = Me.TextBox2.Text
    RS.Fields(2).Value = Me.TextBox3.Text
    RS.Fields(5).Value = Me.TextBox4.Text
    RS.Update()
    MsgBox("Record Saved")
End Sub
``` |
| **Button2 Click** | ```
Private Sub Button2_Click(ByVal sender As Object, ByVal e As _
     System.EventArgs) Handles Button2.Click
    RS.AddNew()
    Button1_Click(sender, e)
    Me.ListBox1.Items.Clear() 'Not: Me.ListBox1.Clear()
    RS.MoveFirst()
    Do Until RS.EOF
       Me.ListBox1.Items.Add(RS.Fields(1).Value
       RS.MoveNext()
    Loop
End Sub
End Class
``` |

Looks familiar, doesn't it? However, there is at least one big difference between VBA-ADO and VSTO-ADO that you must be aware of: The *ADODB.Command* object does not close anymore once it is executed. If you want to use the same object for a different kind of execution, you get a run-time error. Since the *Command* class does not have a *Close()* method, you need to create more instances of the class if you want more executions with the same connection.

Code Example 54: Using ADO's Command Class Twice

VBA	VSTO
'Reference the latest MS ActiveX Data Objects library	'Reference the latest MS ActiveX Data Objects library (located under the COM tab!)
Dim CN As ADODB.Connection Set CN = New ADODB.Connection CN.ConnectionString = "…" CN.Open	Dim CN As ADODB.Connection = New ADODB.Connection CN.ConnectionString = "…" CN.Open
Dim RS As ADODB.Recordset Set RS = New ADODB.Recordset	Dim RS As ADODB.Recordset = New ADODB.Recordset
Dim **CM** As ADODB.Command Set CM = New ADODB.Command	Dim **CM1** As ADODB.Command = New **ADODB.Command** Dim **CM2** As ADODB.Command = New **ADODB.Command**

VBA	VSTO

Set CM.ActiveConnection = CN
CM.CommandText = sSQL1
 	
CM.CommandType = adCmdText
CM.Execute
If … Then
 	
    CM.CommandText = sSQL2
    CM.CommandType = adCmdText
    CM.Execute
End If
 	
Set RS.ActiveConnection = CN
RS.Open CM
	CM1.ActiveConnection = CN
	CM1.CommandText = sSQL1
	
	CM1.CommandType = DODB.CommandTypeEnum.adCmdText
	
	If … Then
	    CM1.Execute()
	    CM2.ActiveConnection = CN
	    CM2.CommandText = sSQL2
	    CM2.CommandType = ADODB.CommandTypeEnum.adCmdText
	    RS = **CM2**.Execute()
	Else
	    RS = **CM1**.Execute()
	End If

We won't go into more ADO details, because you may soon find very convincing reasons for making the transition from ADO to ADO.NET. Why? The next chapter will tell you, and perhaps may sway you.

10.3 And Then There Is ADO.NET

What sets the new *ADO.NET library* apart is a *disconnected* data model. Whereas DAO and ADO remain connected with the database until you close the connection, the new model uses the connection with the database only to retrieve and update records. So there is less network traffic!

All other operations like navigating through the data or adding, changing, and deleting records are done without going back to the source database – that is, in a disconnected state. All of this is possible because ADO.NET has its own database manager, represented by the *DataSet* object. Records are read into the *DataSet*, after which the database is immediately closed and disconnected. The *DataSet* keeps track of changes and exports them back to the source when you decide to update the source database.

Figure 47

Transferring data between database and *DataSet*

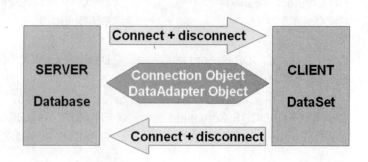

The disconnected data model has many advantages over the older VBA data models where you simply remained in permanent contact with the database:

➤ You can undo or cancel changes until you decide to make them final.

➤ You can program your data manipulation independent of the source database because you have your own database manager (the *DataSet*).

➤ The performance is great once the records have been loaded, which is nice when using laptops or when depending on slow network connections. This model is also fantastic for web applications, because they are not continually connected to their sources.

➤ Of course, it is always wise to limit the amount of information you retrieve from the source database by using SQL statements with WHERE conditions.

➤ As you might expect, there is one big drawback: Other users will not see any changes until the records have been reloaded into the source.

10.3.1 Hard Code by Typing

ADO.NET offers two providers, depending on the type of connection you have chosen: the *OleDb* provider (for databases such as Access) or the *Sql* provider (for databases on SQL Servers). The *OleDb* provider is part of the namespace *System.Data.OleDb*, whereas the *Sql* provider is part of the namespace *System.Data.SqlClient*. In this book, I will focus on *OleDb* databases.

Table 51 Comparing OLE and SQL connections	OLE DB Databases	SQL Servers
	Imports System.Data.**OleDb**	Imports System.Data.**SqlClient**

The disconnected data model is based on three non-visual objects:

OleDbConnection (or *SqlConnection*):
This object establishes a connection to the source database.

OleDbDataAdapter (or *SqlDataAdapter*):
This object does the heavy work of importing and exporting data between the source database and the *DataSet* object. It uses commands to access and modify database records.

Dataset:
This object represents a disconnected set of data. It internally manages— via XML "under the hood" – one or more database tables, which are represented by *DataTable* objects. This is where your disconnected records reside. For sorting and filtering purposes, you can create a *DataView* object, which is a sorted and/or filtered view of a *DataTable* object.

In addition, there are two more rather helpful objects:

🐧 *OleDbCommand:*
This object can manipulate the data coming from the source database by executing SQL statements.

🐧 *OleDbDataReader:*
This object reads the results of a database query. It is capable of efficiently ripping through a group of records – read-only and forward-only. Sometimes that's all you need.

Table 52 Some additional *OleDb* tools	OleDbCommand(sql, CN)	OleDbDataReader
	CM.CommandText	DR.Item
	CM.ExecuteReader(DR)	DR.Read() DR.Close()

What is the structure of a *DataSet*? Well, a *Dataset* contains two collections: *Tables* and *Relations*. The *Relations* collection holds each single relationship between tables. The *Tables* Collection holds all *DataTables*. And each *DataTable* has a collection of *Rows* and *Columns*. What this means, among other things, is that you can access data in any row you specify. That makes quite a difference compared to DAO and ADO, which don't have *Rows* collections, forcing you to use *MoveNext()* and similar move methods to position the recordset to a specific row in order to access its data.

Table 53 *Tables* and *Relations* collections in a *DataSet*	Structure of DataSet	
	DataSet	
	Tables Collection	**Relations** Collection
	(Each) **DataTable**	(Each) **DataRelation**
	Rows Collection **Cols** Collection	

Now we have some important objects, properties, and methods to our avail if we want to manage external databases.

Table 54

Exploring important tools for *OleDb* connections

OleDbConnection("...")	OleDbDataAdapter(sql, CN)	OleDbCommand(sql, CN)	DataSet
CN.ConnectionString = "c:\..."	DA.Connection = CN DA.CommandText = "sql"	CM.Connection = CN CM.CommandText = "sql"	DS.Tables
CN.Open() CN.Close()	DA.Fill(DS, "...") DA.Command(CM) DA.ExecuteReader() DA.Update(DS, "...")		DS.Clear()

Say that you want to create a *Connection* (CN) to *Northwind.mdb* whenever *ThisWorkbook* opens. The *DataAdapter* (DA) transfers records from the database to the *DataSet* (DS) according to a specific SQL *Command* (CM). In this example, CM imports only one field from one specific table. Consequently, the *DataSet* will only hold one table with one field, which you then can read row-by-row into a message box text.

Figure 48

Message box populated from a *DataSet*

Code Example 55: Importing Database Records with ADO.NET into a Message Box

```
Imports System.Data.OleDb

Public Class ThisWorkbook

    Dim CN As New OleDbConnection
    Dim CM As New OleDbCommand
    Dim DA As New OleDbDataAdapter
    Dim DS As New DataSet
    Dim DT As New DataTable

    Private Sub ThisWorkbook_Startup(ByVal sender As Object, _
        ByVal e As System.EventArgs) Handles Me.Startup
    Try
        CN.ConnectionString = "Provider=Microsoft.Jet.OLEDB.4.0;" & _
            "DataSource='C:\Program Files\Microsoft Office\ OFFICE11\'" & _
            "'SAMPLES\Northwind.mdb'"
        CN.Open()
        CM.CommandText = "SELECT CompanyName FROM Suppliers"
        CM.CommandType = CommandType.Text
        CM.Connection = CN
        DA.SelectCommand = CM
        DA.Fill(DS)
        DT = DS.Tables(0)
        Dim txt As String = ""
        For Each DR As DataRow In DT.Rows
            txt = txt & DR.Item(0).ToString & vbCr
        Next
        MsgBox(txt)
    Catch ex As Exception
        MsgBox(ex.Message)
    End Try
    End Sub

End Class
```

Back to the *DataReader*. The *DataReader* is great if you just need to go through the records once, forward and read-only. That's the case when all you need is loading records from an external database into an Excel sheet. Something like the following code would do the job:

Code Example 56: Using ADO's DataReader to Fill a Spreadsheet

```
Imports System.Data.OleDb

Public Class Sheet2

    Private Sub Sheet2_ActivateEvent() Handles Me.ActivateEvent
        Dim CN As New OleDbConnection("Provider=" & _
            "Microsoft.Jet.OLEDB.4.0;" & _
            "Data Source='C:\Program Files\Microsoft Office\'" & _
            "'OFFICE11\SAMPLES\Northwind.mdb'")
        CN.Open()
        Dim SQL As String = "SELECT * FROM Suppliers"
        Dim CM As New OleDbCommand(SQL, CN)
        Dim DR As OleDbDataReader = CM.ExecuteReader
        Dim r As Integer = 1, WS As Excel.Worksheet = _
            CType(Application.ActiveSheet, Excel.Worksheet)
        Do While DR.Read
            For i As Integer = 1 To DR.FieldCount
                WS.Cells(r, i) = DR(i - 1)
            Next
            r += 1
        Loop
        DR.Close()
        CN.Close()
        WS.Columns.AutoFit()
        WS.Rows.AutoFit()
    End Sub

End Class
```

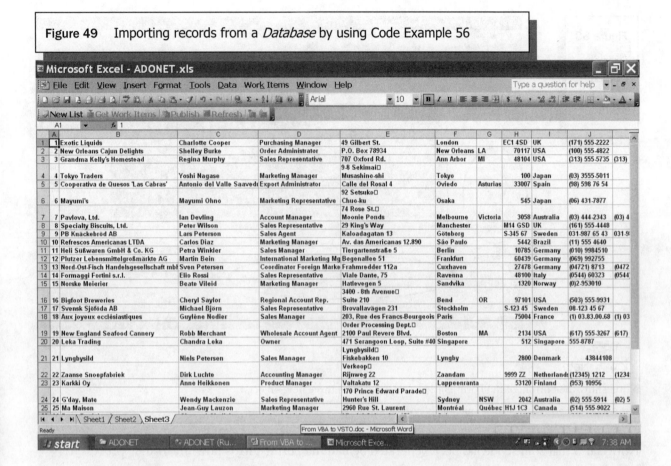

Figure 49   Importing records from a *Database* by using Code Example 56

10.3.2 Automatic Code by Dragging

How do you create all these database objects? The long way is to code everything manually, as we have done so far. A much easier and faster way is to use the Wizards that VB.NET provides.

Table 55	Steps to Take – Data Wizards + DataGridView
Directions for using VB.NET Wizards and DataGridView to create database objects	1. Start a new VB project and call it *DataTools*.
	2. Add a Form: *Project → Add New Item → Windows Form*.
	3. Add a DataSet: *Project → Add New Item → DataSet*.
	4. *View → Server Explorer →* Drag the *Suppliers* table onto the middle screen (*DataSet1.xsd*).
	5. If there is no Database visible in the *Server Explorer*, you need to add one: *Data → Add New Data Source*.
	6. Go back to Form (!) design → Drag *DataSet* from the *Toolbox* (section *Data*) onto the Form → Click *OK*.
	7. Drag a *DataGridView* onto the Form from the *Toolbox* (section *Data*) → Set its *DataSource* to the table *Suppliers* from *DataSet1* (this creates a *SuppliersBindingSource*).

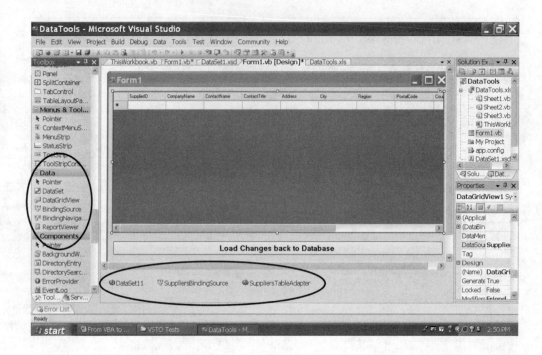

Figure 50

Dragging objects onto a *Form*

   Note:

Notice how the bottom of the Form Design screen features three new objects:

DataSet11, *SuppliersTableAdapter*, and *SuppliersBindingSource*.

Notice also that some code has been generated behind the Form. That's how the loading process has been handled.

```
Public Class Form1

    Private Sub Form1_Load(ByVal sender As System.Object, ByVal e As _
        System.EventArgs) Handles MyBase.Load
        Me.SuppliersTableAdapter.Fill(Me.DataSet11.Suppliers)
    End Sub

End Class
```

Now we want to make sure that the new form gets called somewhere – for instance, in the *Startup* event of *ThisWorkbook*.

```
Public Class ThisWorkbook

    Private Sub ThisWorkbook_Startup(ByVal sender As Object, ByVal e As _
        System.EventArgs) Handles Me.Startup
        Dim WF As New Form1
        WF.Show()
    End Sub

End Class
```

When you run a project like this, it will show you all the records from the *DataSet*, which were imported from the Database. You didn't have to code much! But when you change records, they only change in the *DataSet*. If you want the original database to update as well, the changes in the *DataSet* have to be loaded back into the DataBase. You could do this, for instance, with a *Button* click code.

```
Public Class Form1


    Private Sub Button1_Click(ByVal sender As System.Object, ByVal e As _
        System.EventArgs) Handles Button1.Click
        Me.SuppliersTableAdapter.Update(Me.DataSet11.Suppliers)
    End Sub


End Class
```

Once the above objects have been created, you can find all your data elements in four important screen windows. By the way, be aware that you must run your project first in order to see the new *Data Objects* displayed in the top section of your *Toolbox*.

Figure 51

Data elements displayed in four screen windows

Server Explorer	Toolbox	Solution Explorer	Data Source

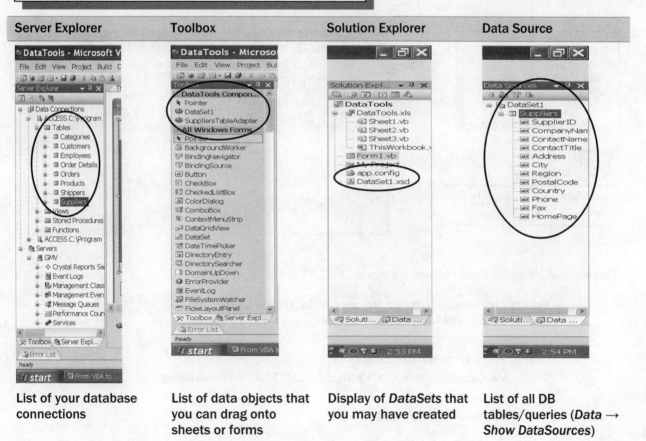

List of your database connections	List of data objects that you can drag onto sheets or forms	Display of *DataSets* that you may have created	List of all DB tables/queries (*Data → Show DataSources*)

Instead of using a *Form* with a *DataGridView*, you can also opt for a *Form* version with *Textboxes*. In this case, you would also want a *BindingNavigator* object, which allows you to navigate from record to record. If you go for this option, you need to take a few more steps, though.

Table 56 Directions for using VB.NET Wizards and Textboxes to create database objects	**Steps to Take – Data Form with Textboxes** 1. Add a new *Form* to the previous project. 2. Drag three objects onto the *Form* from the *Data* section in the *Toolbox*: *DataSet*, *BindingSource*, *BindingNavigator* 3. Set the *DataSource* property of *BindingSource1* to *DataSet1*. 4. Set the *DataMember* property of *BindingSource1* to *Suppliers* (this creates a *SuppliersDataAdapter* again). 5. Set the *BindingSource* property of *BindingNavigator1* to *BindingSource1*. 6. Add a few *Textboxes*. 7. For each *TextBox*, set its *DataBindings Text* (!) property to one of the fields of *DataSet1* (*Text* is under ⊕ *DataBindings*). 8. Make the *Form* pop up when the project runs.

Figure 52 Data form with text boxes	

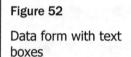

 Note:

Notice how you can navigate from record to record.

You may also want an *Update* button on the form.

```
Private Sub Button1_Click(ByVal sender As System.Object, ByVal e As _
    System.EventArgs) Handles Button1.Click
    Try
        Me.BindingSource1.EndEdit()
        Me.SuppliersTableAdapter.Update(Me.DataSet11.Suppliers)
    Catch ex As Exception
        MsgBox("Update failed")
    End Try
End Sub
```

Now you can take advantage of the power of all the classes behind these new objects.

1.   Open the window for your *DataSet* (in this case, it's called *DataSet1.xsd*).

2.   Notice which tables or queries it holds (in this case, only the table *Suppliers*, because that was our pick earlier).

3.   Here you can insert a new *TableAdapter*, *Query*, or *Relation* between tables — from the *Toolbox* onto the *DataSet*.

New Wizards will kick in, allowing you to even create queries on and between tables.

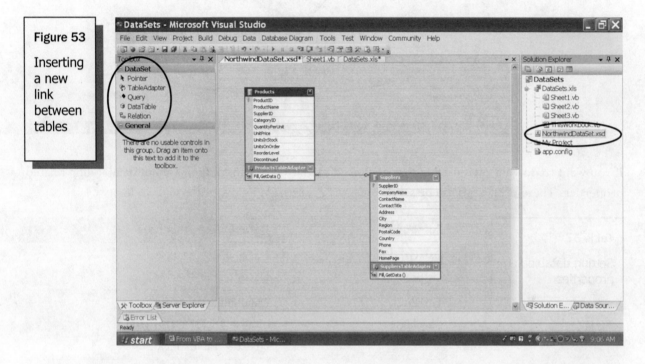

Figure 53

Inserting a new link between tables

4.   Open the window for the *.xls* file.

5.   This time, the *Toolbox* holds a *Components* section (called after your project name). You must run your project first before the components show up.

This section has icons for the *DataSet* and *TableAdapters* that you created in previous steps.

6.   You can drag these objects onto the sheet for use in your code (drag to the sheet itself, not to its bottom section).

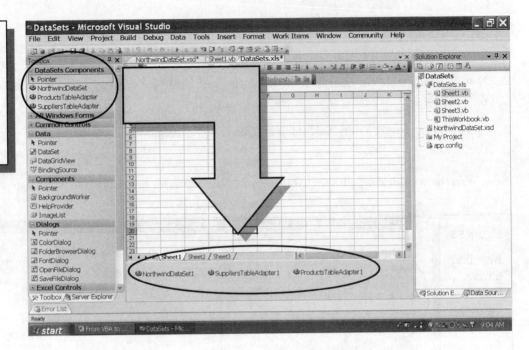

Figure 54

Dragging *DataSet Components* to the Worksheet

If you want to do your own databinding, you need to know a few more things about databinding related properties. These properties can be set through the *Properties* Window or through code.

Table 57

Setting databinding properties

Component	Databinding Properties
DataGridView ListBox	DataSource = DataSet1 DataMember = Table1
TextBox CheckBox	DataBinding Properties: - Tag = Table1.Field1 (ID) - Text = Table1.Field2
ListBox ComboBox	DataSource = DataSet1.Table1 DataMember = Field2 ValueMember = Field1 (ID) SelectedValue = DataSet1.Table2.ID
ListObject	See next chapter (10.4)

One more remark: In general, it is good policy to limit data transfer from table to *DataSet* by using SELECT queries. However, if you did transfer all table records and fields to the *DataSet*, you can still obtain a subset from the *DataSet* by using the *DataView* class, which allows for sorting as well as for row and column filters.

```
Dim myDataView As New DataView(DataSet1.myTable)
myDataView.RowFilter = "Field1='...'"
myDataView.Sort = "Field1, Field3 DESC"
```

If you want to experiment more with creating your own SQL statements, I will give you a few hints to get started.

Table 58	**Steps to Take – Building SQL**
Directions for creating SQL statements	1. *Data → Add New DataSource →* Select your tables. 2. In *Solution Explorer*: Right-click *DataSet → View Designer*. 3. Right-click the header of any table → *Configure*. 4. Button *Query Builder* / Add tables with a right-click if needed. 5. Select or deselect specific fields. 6. In the *Filter* column: Add your criteria (=… / =? / LIKE ?). 7. For calculated fields: Right-click → *Add Group By*. 8. Under *Column*: a name → Under *Alias*: a formula → Under *GroupBy*: *Expression* → Check the SQL statement. 9. Click *OK → Next → Next → Finish*. 10. Right-click on any table → *Preview Data* → Check the results. 11. Once you run the project, you'll also find all of them in the top section of your *Toolbox*. 12. In order to use any of these entities, drag them from the *Toolbox* onto a sheet or form. 13. Dragging them from *Data Sources* instead will create three objects at once: a *DataSet*, *TableAdapter*, and *BindingSource* (visible at the bottom of the middle panel).

10.4 Host Controls Revisited

One of the *Host* controls we discussed earlier (see 3.3) is the *ListObject*. This control is fantastic for database work in Excel because it allows you to create a quick connection to a database table and/or query so the control can display all its records and fields when running an Excel project.

Table 59 Directions for creating a ListObject control	**Steps to Take – Creating a ListObject Control**
	1. Start a new project.
	2. Drag a *Listbox* control onto the 1st sheet: *Toolbox* → section *Excel Controls* → *ListObject*.
	3. Connect this control to cell *A1*.
	4. Go to its *Properties*: *DataSource* → select the dropdown.
	5. If you have already DB connections, you could select one here. If not, click *Add Project DataSource*.
	6. Select *Database* → *Next*.
	7. Press *New Connection* button → browse to *Northwind* database.
	8. Press *Test Connection* → *OK* → *No* (or *Yes*) → *Next*.
	9. Mark ☑ *Tables* (or one of them) → *Finish*.
	10. Go back to *DataSource* property and select one table. Now the control will get filled nicely with field headers.
	11. Finally the test: *Debug* → *Start*.

You will be surprised to see how swiftly this *ListObject* control works. It lists all the records that were transferred from the table or query to the dataset.

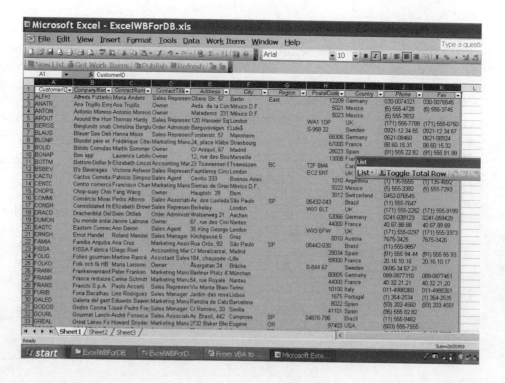

Figure 55

Using *Host Control*s to import records

A lot of work was done for you in the background. You will notice in the design view of *Sheet1* that three new objects were added to the bottom of the screen: a *NorthWindDataSet*, a *CustomersBindingSource*, and a *CustomersTableAdapter*. Each one is a specific instance of its class.

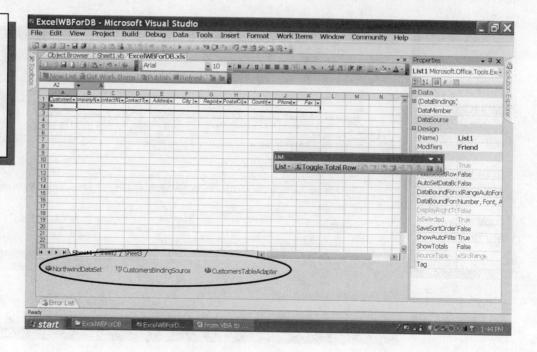

Figure 56

Dragging *DataSet Components* to the Worksheet

There are actually two different ways of automatically populating a *ListObject*. The main difference is whether you create a *DataSet* before or after you implement the *ListObject*. Here is a summary:

Table 60 Comparing ways of automatically populating a ListObject	**Start with ListObject**	**Start with Data Source**
	1. Drag a *ListObject* from the *Toolbox* onto the sheet.	1. *Data / Add New DataSource /* Select >= 1 table / Finish the process.
	2. *Data / Add New DataSource /* Select >=1 table / Finish the process.	2. Data / Show DataSources. Click the dropdown of your source.
	3. Open the *Properties* box of the *ListObject*.	3. Select ListObject.
	4. Set property *DataSource* to the new *DataSet*.	4. Drag the *Data Source* onto the sheet.
	5. Set property *DataMember* to one of its tables.	5. All *Property* settings are done for you.
	6. Check the sheet's code.	6. Check the sheet's code.

In case you wonder what happened in the background, right-click on any of these new objects at the bottom of the screen and select *View Code*. There you will see the code that was added during the design process. This is the place, of course, where you can also insert your own code.

Figure 57

The *TableAdapter* gets filled automatically with one of the tables from the *DataSet* – thanks to the code shown at right:

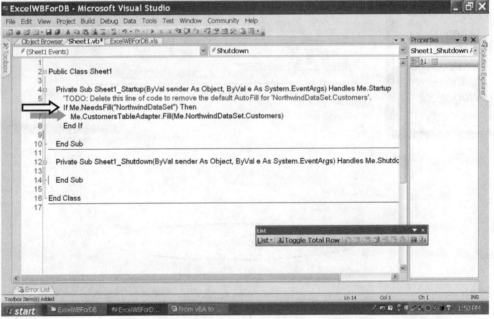

If you want to regulate anything in addition to what the *Designer* has done for you, you would need some additional code. For instance, let's say that you wish to send changes made in the *ListObject* control back to the database "on the server." Remember, we are dealing with a disconnected database. That allows you to use the *Sheet1_ShutDown* event for this purpose and call the *TableAdapter*'s *Update()* method.

```
Me.CustomersTableAdapter.Update(Me.NorthwindDataSet)
```

Thanks to the *Update()* method, any changes made in the *DataSet* persist in the Database when you close the sheet and open it again. Obviously, there are other ways of updating the database – for instance, by using timers, buttons, etc.

It is also possible to insert code for regulating the appearance of this new *ListObject*. Say you want to use the *AutoFit* method for the rows and columns of *List1*.

```
Private Sub Sheet1_Startup(ByVal sender As Object, ByVal e As System.EventArgs) _
    Handles Me.Startup
    If Me.NeedsFill("DataSet1") Then
        Me.SuppliersTableAdapter.Fill(Me.DataSet1.Suppliers)
        Dim myRange As Excel.Range = Me.List1.DataBodyRange
        myRange.EntireColumn.AutoFit()
        myRange.EntireRow.AutoFit()
    End If
End Sub
```

 Note:

Lighter colored text in code samples indicates code that was automatically inserted by VSTO.

Let's study one more situation – that is, when you want to create a filter for your *ListObject*'s table. In a case like this, we could use a *NamedRange* object in addition to a *ListObject*. When users type one or more characters in the *NamedRange* object, the *ListObject* shows only records of companies whose name begins with those characters. In order to do so, you would need two separate *TableAdapters* – one for a complete table listing and one for a filtered table listing.

Figure 58

Creating a *ListObject* with filter capabilities

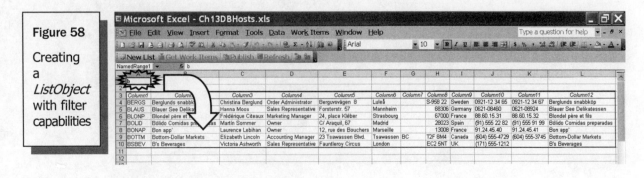

<table>
<tr><td>

Table 61

Directions for creating a Listbox with filtering capabilities

</td><td>

Steps to Take – Creating a ListObject with Filter Capabilities

1.   Drag a *NamedRange* object onto a sheet (cell *A1*).

2.   Create a *ListObject* (in *A3*) connected to the *Customers* table.

3.   Run the project – this should populate the total list.
     Notice the four new objects at the bottom of the sheet design.

Now it is time to create a second *CustomersTableAdapter*, but this time with a filter.

4.   *Data → Show Data Sources →* right-click on your source *→ Edit DataSet With Designer*.
     This opens *NorthwindDataset.xsd*.

5.   Right-click in middle panel *→ Add → TableAdapter*.

6.   In Wizard: *Next →* ⊙ *Use SQL → Next →* Button *Query Builder*.

7.   In Builder: *Customers → Add →* ☑ * *(All) →* ☑ *CompanyName*.

8.   Type in the *Filter* column for row 2: LIKE ?

9.   Click *OK* / check the SQL statement *→ Next → Next → Finish*.

Notice the second *TableAdapter*: *Customers1TableAdapter*.
After you run the project, you will find the second *TableAdapter* in the *Toolbox* (top section).

10. Drag it from the *Toolbox* to the bottom of the sheet.

11. Now you can use it in your code so the list only shows company names starting with what is typed in cell A1.

</td></tr>
</table>

Code Example 57: Creating a ListObject with Filter Capabilities

```
Public Class Sheet1

    Private Sub Sheet1_Startup(ByVal sender As Object, ByVal e _
        As System.EventArgs) Handles Me.Startup
        If Me.NeedsFill("NorthwindDataSet") Then
            Me.CustomersTableAdapter.Fill(Me.NorthwindDataSet.Customers)
        End If
        Dim CR As Excel.Range = CType(List1.DataBodyRange, Excel.Range)
        CR.EntireColumn.AutoFit()
    End Sub


    Private Sub NamedRange1_Change(ByVal Target As _
        Microsoft.Office.Interop.Excel.Range) Handles NamedRange1.Change
        Dim sFilter As String = Target.Value.ToString & "%"
        List1.DataMember = "Customers1"
        If Me.NeedsFill("NorthwindDataSet") Then
            Me.Customers1TableAdapter1.Fill( Me.NorthwindDataSet.Customers1, sFilter)
        End If
        Dim CR As Excel.Range = CType(List1.DataBodyRange, Excel.Range)
        CR.EntireColumn.AutoFit()
    End Sub

End Class
```

It is good to know that you can also drag single *Fields* from the *Data Source* box onto your sheet. Single fields won't hook up to a *ListObject* but rather to a *NamedRange*. When you drag them to a specific cell on the sheet, the properties *DataSource* and *DataMember* are automatically assigned for each *NamedRange*.

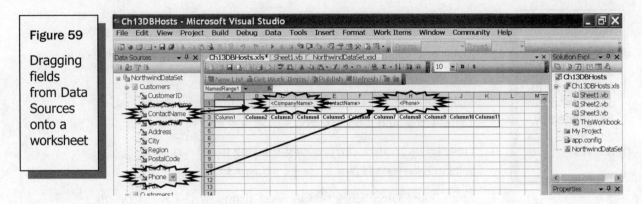

Figure 59

Dragging fields from Data Sources onto a worksheet

However, each *NamedRange* box will only show data for the first record in the *BindingSource*. To display other data, you need to gather information from another position in the *BindingSource*. Say, the user has clicked on another record in the *ListObject* below the *NamedRanges*, and now wants to see only the information for that specific record. The following code would achieve this:

```
Private Sub List1_SelectedIndexChanged(ByVal sender As Object, ByVal e As _
    System.EventArgs) Handles List1.SelectedIndexChanged
    Me.CustomersBindingSource.Position = Me.List1.SelectedIndex - 1
End Sub
```

Let's go back to the *ActionsPane*, which we discussed earlier (see 7.4). An *ActionsPane* can also hold so-called *UserControls*. And a *UserControl*, in turn, can hold something like a database connection. Let's study the following example: A Worksheet holds two elements – a *ListObject* that shows all table records plus a panel to its left that displays the detailed information of a specific record. Selecting a different record in the *ListObject* should update the information in the panel, and navigating to a different record in the panel selects the corresponding record in the *ListObject*. In other words, both elements are synchronized!

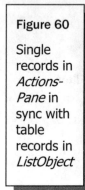

Figure 60

Single records in *Actions-Pane* in sync with table records in *ListObject*

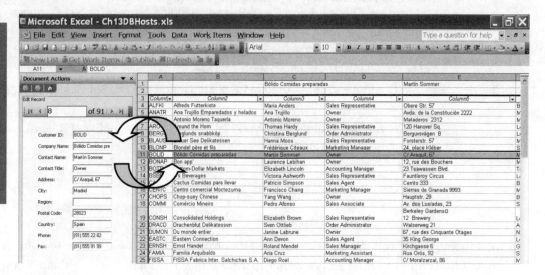

Table 62

Directions for using the ActionsPane to update and to be updated by database records

Steps to Take – ActionsPane for Database Records

1. Make sure you have a project with a *ListObject* showing some table (e.g. *Customers*).

2. Make sure the sheet shows at the bottom three objects: a *DataSet*, *TableAdapter*, and *BindingSource*.

3. First, let us create a *UserControl* displaying the first record. Select *Project → Add New Item → UserControl*.

4. From *Data Sources*: Click on *Customers'* dropdown → Select *Details*.

5. Now drag *Customers* onto the control so all textboxes, labels, and a navigator get automatically implemented.

6. Add this *UserControl* to the *ActionsPane* with this code:

Code Example 58: Creating an ActionsPane for Database Records

```
Public Class ThisWorkbook

    Public myUC As New UserControl1

    Private Sub ThisWorkbook_Startup(ByVal sender As Object, ByVal e _
        As System.EventArgs) Handles Me.Startup
      Dim CB As Office.CommandBar = Me.Application.CommandBars("Task Pane")
      CB.Width = 300
      CB.Position = Microsoft.Office.Core.MsoBarPosition.msoBarLeft
      Me.ActionsPane.Controls.Add(myUC)
    End Sub

End Class
```

Now we need to make sure that the *UserControl* loads properly.

Code Example 59: Loading UserControl

```
Public Class UserControl1

    Private Sub UserControl1_Load(ByVal sender As System.Object, ByVal e _
        As System.EventArgs) Handles MyBase.Load
      Me.BackColor = Color.Ivory
      Me.Size = New Size(200, 400)
      Me.CustomersTableAdapter.Fill(Me.NorthwindDataSet.Customers)
    End Sub

End Class
```

In the *Sheet*'s code, you want to update the position of the *BindingSource* according to what has been selected in the *ListBox*. The following code should do the job.

Code Example 60: Updating BindingSource position

```
Public Class Sheet1

    Private Sub Sheet1_Startup(ByVal sender As Object, ByVal e _
        As System.EventArgs) Handles Me.Startup
      If Me.NeedsFill("NorthwindDataSet") Then
        Me.CustomersTableAdapter.Fill(Me.NorthwindDataSet.Customers)
      End If
      Dim CR As Excel.Range = CType(List1.DataBodyRange, Excel.Range)
      CR.EntireColumn.AutoFit()
      CR.EntireRow.AutoFit()
    End Sub

    Private Sub List1_SelectedIndexChanged(ByVal sender As Object, ByVal e _
        As System.EventArgs) Handles List1.SelectedIndexChanged
      Me.CustomersBindingSource.Position = Me.List1.SelectedIndex - 1
```

```
            Globals.ThisWorkbook.myUC.CustomersBindingSource.Position = _
                Me.List1.SelectedIndex - 1
        End Sub

    End Class
```

Now you must make sure that record navigation gets updated throughout the system and highlight the corresponding record in the *ListObject*.

Code Example 61: Updating Record Navigation

```
    Public Class UserControl1

        Private Sub CustomersBindingSource_CurrentChanged(ByVal sender As _
            Object, ByVal e As System.EventArgs) Handles _
            CustomersBindingSource.CurrentChanged
        Try
            Globals.Sheet1.List1.AutoSelectRows = True
            Globals.Sheet1.List1.SelectedIndex = Me.CustomersBindingSource.Position + 1
        Catch ex As Exception

        End Try
        End Sub
    End Class
```

To cut a long story short, it is certainly possible to manipulate databases merely from home-made code, but it is usually much easier to get started by dragging controls onto your sheets or forms. That is one of the big advantages of using ADO.NET over ADO. And that's why I will not pay any more attention to creating code completely from scratch. But go ahead if you feel differently.

10.5 Dynamic Forms

You may want to create *Forms* on the fly, especially when working with databases – with as many textboxes and labels as a particular table or query has fields. This makes your *Form* more universal and adaptable to changing situations.

That's exactly what I tried to do with the following code. The underlying *Form* has only a few controls created at design time. The rest will be produced and added at run-time after the user has decided – by way of a *ComboBox* – which table from the *DataSet* should be displayed. There are four buttons on top of the form to allow the user to navigate through the records of each table, once the corresponding table has been loaded.

Figure 61   Forms created by the same code

Form 2		Form 2	
Employees ▾ «« « » »»		Products ▾ «« « » »»	
EmployeeID	1	ProductID	1
LastName	Davolio	ProductN;	Chai
FirstName	Nancy	SupplierID	1
Title	Sales Representative	CategoryII	1
TitleOfCourt:	Ms.	QuantityP;	10 boxes x 20 bags
BirthDate	12/8/1968 12:00:00 AM	UnitPrice	18
HireDate	5/1/1992 12:00:00 AM	UnitsInSto	39
Address	507 - 20th Ave. E.□□Apt. 2A	UnitsOnOr	0
City	Seattle	ReorderLe	10
Region	WA	Discontinu	False
PostalCode	98122		
Country	USA		
HomePhone	(206) 555-9857		
Extension	5467		
Photo	EmpID1.bmp		
Notes	Education includes a BA in psycholog		
ReportsTo	2		

Same form design

Table 63	**Steps to Take – Forms with same design and user-selectable controls**
Directions for creating different forms based on the same code	1. Start a new Project and add a new *Windows Form*. 2. Place on the *Form*: One *ComboBox*, one *LabelBox*, one *TextBox*, and four *Buttons* (the rest is done at run-time). 3. Create a data source: *Data → Add New DataSource → Database → Next*. 4. Choose or find *Northwind* (again) → click *Next → Next* 5. Choose for your *DataSet* only the tables ☑*Customers*, ☑ *Employees*, ☑*Categories*, ☑ *Products*, and ☑ *Suppliers*. 6. Accept the *DataSet* name and click *Finish*. 7. From *View → Data Sources*: Drag each table onto the *Form* (!) and delete each *Listbox* that was automatically added. 8. The *Form* now features some 11 new objects at the bottom. 9. Empty ALL *Form*'s code and replace it with your own code:

Code Example 62: Creating Dynamic Forms to Display Imported Tables of Various Sizes

```vb
Public Class Form1

    Dim sTable As String

    Private Sub Form1_Load(ByVal sender As Object, ByVal e _
        As System.EventArgs) Handles Me.Load
        'Replace what was in here with this code:

        For i As Integer = 0 To Me.NorthwindDataSet.Tables.Count - 1
            Me.ComboBox1.Items.Add(Me.NorthwindDataSet.Tables(i).TableName)
        Next
    End Sub


    Private Sub ComboBox1_SelectedValueChanged(ByVal sender As Object, ByVal _
        e As System.EventArgs) Handles ComboBox1.SelectedValueChanged
        Dim LB As Label, TB As TextBox
        sTable = Me.ComboBox1.Text
        With Me.NorthwindDataSet.Tables(sTable)
            Me.Label1.Text = .Columns(0).ColumnName
            Me.Label1.Width = 40
            Me.Label1.Font = New Font("Arial", 12, FontStyle.Bold)
            Me.TextBox1.Font = New Font("Arial", 12, FontStyle.Bold)
            Me.TextBox1.DataBindings.Clear()
            Me.TextBox1.DataBindings.Add(New System.Windows.Forms.Binding_
                ("Text", Me.NorthwindDataSet, sTable _
                & "." & .Columns(0).ColumnName))
            For i As Integer = Me.Controls.Count - 1 To 7 Step -1
                Me.Controls(i).Dispose()
            Next
            For i As Integer = 1 To .Columns.Count - 1
                LB = New Label
                LB.Left = Me.Label1.Left
                LB.Width = Me.Label1.Width
                LB.Font = New Font("Arial", 12, FontStyle.Bold)
                LB.Top = Me.Label1.Top + CInt(Me.Label1.Height * 2 * i)
                LB.Text = .Columns(i).ColumnName
                TB = New TextBox
                TB.ReadOnly = True
                TB.Left = Me.TextBox1.Left
                TB.Width = Me.TextBox1.Width
                TB.Font = New Font("Arial", 12, FontStyle.Bold)
                TB.Top = Me.Label1.Top + CInt(Me.Label1.Height * 2 * i)
                TB.DataBindings.Add(New System.Windows.Forms.Binding_
                    ("Text", Me.NorthwindDataSet, sTable & "." _
                    & .Columns(i).ColumnName))
```

```
            Me.Controls.Add(LB)
            Me.Controls.Add(TB)
        Next
        Me.NorthwindDataSet.Clear()
        Select Case sTable
            Case "Categories"
                Me.CategoriesTableAdapter.Fill(Me.NorthwindDataSet.Categories)
            Case "Employees"
                Me.EmployeesTableAdapter.Fill (Me.NorthwindDataSet.Employees)
            Case "Customers"
                Me.CustomersTableAdapter.Fill (Me.NorthwindDataSet.Customers)
            Case "Products"
                Me.ProductsTableAdapter.Fill (Me.NorthwindDataSet.Products)
            Case "Suppliers"
                Me.SuppliersTableAdapter.Fill (Me.NorthwindDataSet.Suppliers)
        End Select
    End With
End Sub


Private Sub Button1_Click(ByVal sender As System.Object, ByVal e _
    As System.EventArgs) Handles Button1.Click
    With Me.BindingContext(Me.NorthwindDataSet, sTable)
        Try
            .Position = 0
        Catch ex As Exception
            .CancelCurrentEdit()
        End Try
    End With
End Sub


Private Sub Button2_Click(ByVal sender As Object, ByVal e As _
    System.EventArgs) Handles Button2.Click
    With Me.BindingContext(Me.NorthwindDataSet, sTable)
        Try
            .Position = .Position - 1
        Catch ex As Exception
            .CancelCurrentEdit()
        End Try
    End With
End Sub


Private Sub Button3_Click(ByVal sender As Object, ByVal e As _
    System.EventArgs) Handles Button3.Click
    With Me.BindingContext(Me.NorthwindDataSet, sTable)
        Try
```

```
            .Position = .Position + 1
        Catch ex As Exception
            .CancelCurrentEdit()
        End Try
    End With
End Sub

Private Sub Button4_Click(ByVal sender As Object, ByVal e As _
        System.EventArgs) Handles Button4.Click
    With Me.(Me.NorthwindDataSet, sTable)
        Try
            .Position = .Count - 1
        Catch ex As Exception
            .CancelCurrentEdit()
        End Try
    End With
End Sub
End Class
```

```
Public Class ThisWorkbook

    Private Sub ThisWorkbook_Startup(ByVal sender As Object, ByVal e As _
            System.EventArgs) Handles Me.Startup
        Dim WF As New Form1
        WF.Show()
    End Sub

End Class
```

10.6 Case Study: A Rosetta Stone

Figure 62

Form that uses first data grid as a filter for the second data grid

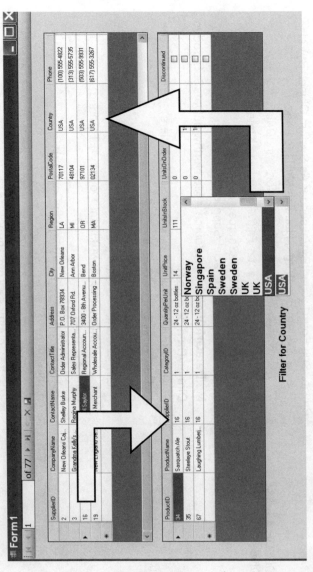

For this case study, we will design a form that has ADO.NET behind it - instead of the "older" ADO Library. The first *DataGridView* allows users to filter for records in the second *DataGridView*. Besides, there is a filter for a specific Country.

1. Create a NEW Excel project, name it ADONET, and save it.

2. Add a *Windows Form* with two *DataGridViews* (from the section *Data*) and don't worry about their *DataSource* (the code handle this).

3. Add also one *Combobox* (from the section *Common Controls*).

4. Create a data source: *Data → Add New DataSource → Database → Next.*

5. Choose or find *Northwind* (again) → click *Next → Next.*

6. Choose the tables ☑ *Products* and ☑ *Suppliers* (for your *DataSet*).

7. Accept the *DataSet* name and click *Finish.*

8. From *View → Data Sources*: Drag *Products* onto the *Form* (not onto the *DataGridView*) and delete the *Listbox* that came with it. The *Form* now features three new objects at the bottom: a *DataSet*, a *BindingSource*, and a *TableAdapter.*

9. Repeat the same process for the *Suppliers* table. Notice that the *Form's Load* code has been created for you.

10. Now add your own VSTO code (much shorter than its VBA version).

Code Example 63: Using a DataGridView with ADO.NET

VBA Version	VSTO Version

VBA Version

```
'In UserForm1

Dim CN As New ADODB.Connection
Dim CM As New ADODB.Command
Dim RS As New ADODB.Recordset

Private Sub UserForm_Activate()
    Set CN = New ADODB.Connection
    CN.ConnectionString = "Provider=Microsoft.Jet.OLEDB.4.0;" & _
        "Data Source='C:\Program Files\Microsoft Office\" & _
        "OFFICE11\SAMPLES\Northwind.mdb'"
    CN.Open
    Set CM = New ADODB.Command
    Set CM.ActiveConnection = CN
    CM.CommandType = adCmdText
    CM.CommandText = "SELECT * From Suppliers"
    CM.Execute
    Set RS = New ADODB.Recordset
    Set RS.ActiveConnection = CN
    RS.Open CM, , adOpenStatic
    Do Until RS.EOF
        txt = ""
        For i = 0 To RS.Fields.Count - 1
            txt = txt & RS.Fields(i).Value & vbTab
        Next
```

VSTO Version

```
Public Class Form1

Private Sub Form1_Load(ByVal sender As System.Object, ByVal _
    e As System.EventArgs) Handles MyBase.Load
    Me.SuppliersTableAdapter.Fill(Me.NorthwindDataSet.Suppliers)
    Me.ProductsTableAdapter.Fill(Me.NorthwindDataSet.Products)
    Me.DataGridView1.DataSource = _
        Me.NorthwindDataSet.Suppliers
    Me.DataGridView2.DataSource = Me.NorthwindDataSet.Products
    Dim myDataView As New _
        DataView (Me.NorthwindDataSet.Suppliers)
    myDataView.Sort = "Country"
    For i As Integer = 0 To myDataView.Count - 1
        Dim sCountry As String = _
            Trim(myDataView(i).Item("Country").ToString)
        If i = 0 Then
            Me.ComboBox1.Items.Add(sCountry)
        Else
            sTrim = Trim(myDataView(i - 1).Item ("Country").ToString)
            If sCountry <> Trim Then
                Me.ComboBox1.Items.Add(sCountry)
```

VSTO Version

```
        End If
      End If
    Next
End Sub
```

VBA Version

```
    Me.ListBox1.AddItem txt
    RS.MoveNext
Loop

CM.CommandText = "SELECT * From Products"
CM.Execute
RS.Requery
Do Until RS.EOF
    txt = ""
    For i = 0 To RS.Fields.Count - 1
        txt = txt & RS.Fields(i).Value & vbTab
    Next
    Me.ListBox2.AddItem txt
    RS.MoveNext
Loop

CM.CommandText = "SELECT Country From Suppliers" & _
    " ORDER BY Country"
CM.Execute
RS.Requery
If IsNull(RS.Fields(0).Value) Then prev = "" Else prev = _
    Trim(RS.Fields(0).Value)
Me.ComboBox1.AddItem prev
RS.MoveNext
Do Until RS.EOF
    cur = Trim(RS.Fields(0).Value)
    If cur <> prev Then Me.ComboBox1.AddItem cur
    prev = cur
    RS.MoveNext
```

VBA Version	VSTO Version

VBA Version

```
        Loop
    End Sub

Private Sub ListBox1_Click()
    Me.ListBox2.Clear
    CM.CommandText = "SELECT * From Products WHERE" & _
        " SupplierID=" & Val(Left(Me.ListBox1.Text, 2))
    CM.Execute
    RS.Requery
    Do Until RS.EOF
        txt = ""
        For i = 0 To RS.Fields.Count - 1
            txt = txt & RS.Fields(i).Value & vbTab
        Next
        Me.ListBox2.AddItem txt
        RS.MoveNext
    Loop
End Sub

Private Sub ComboBox1_Click()
    Me.ListBox1.Clear
    CM.CommandText = "SELECT * From Suppliers WHERE" & _
        " Country='" & Me.ComboBox1.Text & "'"
    CM.Execute
    RS.Requery
    Do Until RS.EOF
        txt = ""
        For i = 0 To RS.Fields.Count – 1
```

VSTO Version

```
Private Sub DataGridView1_CellClick(ByVal _
    sender As Object, ByVal e As _
    System.Windows.Forms.DataGridViewCellEventArgs) _
    Handles DataGridView1.CellClick

    Dim myDataView As New _
        DataView(Me.NorthwindDataSet.Products)

    myDataView.RowFilter = "SupplierID=" & _
        Me.DataGridView1.Item(0, e.RowIndex).Value.ToString
    Me.DataGridView2.DataSource = myDataView
End Sub

Private Sub ComboBox1_SelectedValueChanged(ByVal _
    sender As Object, ByVal e As System.EventArgs) _
    Handles ComboBox1.SelectedValueChanged

    Dim myDataView As New _
        DataView (Me.NorthwindDataSet.Suppliers)

    myDataView.RowFilter = "Country='" & _
        Me.ComboBox1.Text & ""
    Me.DataGridView1.DataSource = myDataView

    myDataView = New DataView(Me.NorthwindDataSet.Products)
    myDataView.RowFilter = "SupplierID=" & _
```

VBA Version

```
    txt = txt & RS.Fields(i).Value & vbTab
  Next
  Me.ListBox1.AddItem txt
  RS.MoveNext
 Loop
End Sub
```

```
'In Module

Sub OpenForm()
 UserForm1.Show vbModal
End Sub
```

VSTO Version

```
    Me.DataGridView1.Item(0, 0).Value.ToString
    Me.DataGridView2.DataSource = myDataView
  End Sub

End Class
```

```
Public Class ThisWorkbook

 Private Sub ThisWorkbook_Startup(ByVal sender As Object, ByVal _
   e As System.EventArgs) Handles Me.Startup
   Dim WF As New Form1
   WF.Show()
 End Sub

End Class
```

11 Building Your Own Classes

11.1 New Elements

VBA used to have separate code sections for Excel objects (such as sheets), for modules (such as macros), userforms, and, last but not least, for classes. To use five classes in a VBA project, you would need five different class modules. In VSTO, however, all these class sections can be combined in a single class module. And ultimately, all separate code sections will be united into a single source file called *Assembly*.

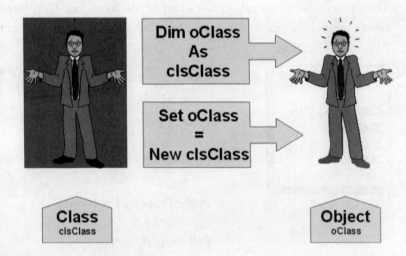

Figure 63

Creating Objects as instances of Classes

Create a Class (a template for Objects)	Create an Object (an instance of a Class)
➤ Properties	➤ Declare variable
➤ Methods and Functions	➤ Create Object
➤ Events	➤ Use its Class

Table 64

Creating Classes and creating Objects

To start your own class, you first declare a *Public Class* and then declare some internal variables based on encapsulation. Encapsulation protects your private variables from being used directly by the "world" outside of the class.

Figure 64

Declaring private variables protects your class variables from being used directly by the outside world

Then you create some properties – just as you would in VBA. But notice that the property skeleton has been changed: No more *Get* and *Let/Set*, but *Get* and *Set* only, plus they have been combined inside one *Property* declaration.

Table 65

Comparing VBA and VSTO property skeletons

VBA	VSTO
	Public Property Name() …
Public Property **Get** Name() …	**Get**
…	…
End Property	**End Get**
Public Property **Let** Name(…)	**Set** (…)
…	…
End Property	**End Set**
	End Property

If you just want a read-only property, use the *ReadOnly* keyword: *Public ReadOnly Property() As …* – and do not include a *Set* section. A similar story goes for write-only properties.

```
Public Class myClass

        Private m_sName as String

        Public Property Name() As String
                Get
                        Name = m_sName
                End Get
                Set (ByVal str As String)
                        m_sName = str
                End Set
        End Property

End Class
```

In addition to properties, you can also add your own methods and functions to the class. Nothing has really changed here in VSTO – except that you can use the *Return* keyword inside a function instead of using its function name again. And parameters are passed *ByVal* as a default, whereas VBA used *ByRef* as a default (see 4.2).

```
Public Class myClass

    Public Sub myMethod()
        ...
    End Sub

    Public Function myFunction() As Integer
        ...
    End Function

End Class
```

| ```
Function myFunction(i As Integer)
    myFunction = i * i
End Function
``` | ```
Function myFunction(i As Integer)
    Return i * i
End Function
``` |

In connection with methods, we should mention the issue of "overloading" again (see 4.2). That's where the keyword *Overloads* comes in.

| O V E R L O A D I N G | ```
Overloads Function Min(ByVal X As Double,
ByVal Y As Double) As Double
        Min = IIf(X < Y, X, Y)
End Function
``` |
| | ```
Overloads Function Min(ByVal X As String,
ByVal Y As String) As String
        Min = IIf(X < Y, X, Y)
End Function
``` |
| | ```
Overloads Function Min(ByVal X As Date,
ByVal Y As Date) As Date
        Min = IIf(X < Y, X, Y)
End Function
``` |

All classes have a *New()* method in VSTO – comparable to the class' *Initialize* event in VBA. With this method, you can set default starting values and such. Needless to say, *Overloading* allows you to choose between accepting a default value and setting a specific value.

```
Public Class myClass

    m_iValue as Integer

    Public Overloads Sub New()
        m_iValue = 100
    End Sub
```
```

```
            Public Overloads Sub New(ByVal val As Integer)
                  m_iValue = val
            End Sub

      End Class
```

If you like to use the same class name for different classes, you can assign a specific *namespace* to each class. When calling the class, the namespace obviously has to be included.

```
      Namespace myName

            Public Class myClass

            End Class

      End Namespace

      Private oClass As myName.myClass
```

For those of you who like to add *Events* to your classes, things have not changed much. The only big difference is that you can use any name for your event handler, but you must use the keyword *Handles* and the *Name* of the class' event. Consequently, one event handler can handle multiple events, and one event can be used by several event handlers (see 4.3).

Table 66

Comparing VBA and VSTO event handler codes

VBA	VSTO
Public Class myClass Public Event **myEvt**()	Public Class myClass Public Event **myEvt**()

Public Sub myMethod
    RaiseEvent **myEvt**
End Sub
	Public Sub myMethod
	    RaiseEvent **myEvt**
	End Sub

End Class	End Class
Dim WithEvents **myObj** As myClass (Set oVar = New myClass)	Dim WithEvents **myObj** As myClass = _ New myClass()

Private Sub **myObj_myEvt**()
    MsgBox …
End Sub
	Private Sub AnyName() **Handles myObj.myEvt**
	    MsgBox(…)
	End Sub

How do you examine class objects for equality? Because class objects are of the *Reference* type, you need the *Is* keyword (see 5.1). But the next step depends on whether you want to check for equal instances or equal types.

Table 67 Checking for equal instances vs. equal types	Equal instances	Equal types
	If oA **Is** oB Then …	If oA.**GetType**() **Is** oB.**GetType**() Then …

Once a *Class* has been created in a Class module, we want to create *Objects* (as instances of this Class) in any other module – so we can use their properties, methods, and events. The creation of *Objects* can be done in one or two steps: You can separate their declaration and creation, or you can combine them into one step.

Table 68 Combining or separating an Object's declaration and creation	Two steps	Declare	Dim myObj As myClass
			myObj.myMethod(…)
		Create	myObj = **New** myClass()
			myObj.myMethod(…)
	One step	Declare and Create	Dim myObj As **New** myClass myObj.myMethod(…)
		Declare and Create	Dim myObj As myClass = **New** myClass() myObj.myMethod(…)

11.2 Real Inheritance

VB was supposed to be an *Object-Oriented* programming language (OOP) – but it wasn't in the full sense. VB.NET, on the other hand, truly is *Object-Oriented* because it uses and allows real inheritance.

Inheritance has to be distinguished from *Containment*. *Containment* is often called a "has-a" relationship – for instance, an invoice "has a" line item. *Inheritance*, on the other hand, is often called an "is-a" relationship – for instance, a product item "is-a" line item, and so is a service item. Through inheritance, you can specify items with more and more detail.

Inheritance is what most classes are based on. The base-class or parent-class harbors the common functionality, whereas the sub-classes or child-classes extend this common functionality from the base-class with specific functionality. Sub-classes inherit the behavior of base-classes and become more and more specific (see 3.1). This allows you to create your own hierarchies of parent-classes and child-classes. Through the use of inheritance, the child-class builds on or inherits the functionality of the parent-class. The keyword here is *Inherits*.

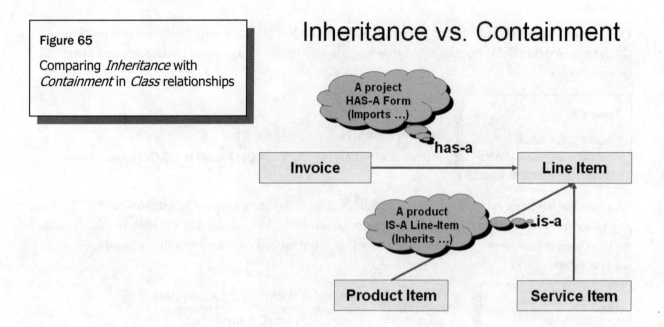

Figure 65

Comparing *Inheritance* with *Containment* in *Class* relationships

To create child-classes, you need to use the *Inherits* keyword inside your child-class declaration.

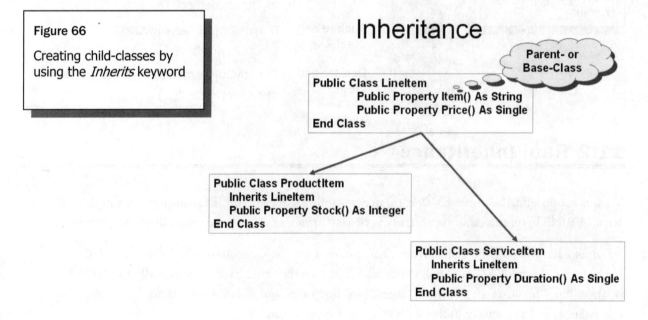

Figure 66

Creating child-classes by using the *Inherits* keyword

You can further specialize the child-class by replacing or overriding some functionality of the parent-class, so the specialized class can act just like the parent-class in some situations but different in other situations. To allow this behavior, you need the *Overridable* keyword in the parent-class plus the *Overrides* keyword in the child-class.

```
Public Class Parent
     Public Overridable Function myFunction() As String
          …
     End Function
End Class
```

```
Public Class Child Inherits Parent
     Overrides Function myFunction() As String
          …
     End Function
End Class
```

There is much more to classes, which we will leave for more specialized books on VB.NET.

11.3 Garbage Collection

In VBA, an object was destroyed when its last reference was removed. This approach was implemented through reference counting. So it was always clear when an object would be terminated, triggering a call to its *Class_Terminate* event. In VSTO, however, reference counting has been replaced with so-called *garbage collection*: At certain times, the system will run through all objects looking for those that no longer have any references. Those objects are then terminated – the garbage collected by triggering the *Class_Finalize* event.

In other words, we don't know exactly when an object will really be destroyed in VSTO. Once all references have been eliminated, objects will just hang around in memory until the garbage collection performs a cleanup. You can take decisions into your own hand by using the class' *Dispose*() method.

What is the advantage of garbage collection? We won't go into all its details except for mentioning the fact that it eliminates circular reference issues found with reference counting. If two objects have references to each other and there are no references to either object left, the garbage collector will discover and terminate them, whereas VBA would have left them in memory forever. Another advantage is that garbage collection takes place when the application is otherwise idle, thus not interfering with overall performance.

Let's say we want to create a class that handles bank transactions for a bank account. What we would need is a *Class* plus a *Form* that uses this new *Class*. We could do much more – for instance, creating a collection of bank accounts, and then saving to disk the information for all accounts (as we did in 9.2). But this time, we will leave that part up to you.

11.4 Case Study: A Rosetta Stone

Figure 67

Recording bank account transactions using a Form

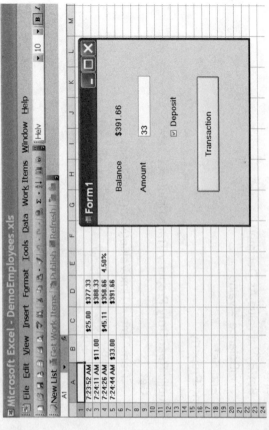

The following Project holds a *Class* that handles basic transactions for a bank account: withdrawals, deposits, and interest payments. The class supplies all the necessary business logic.

The Project also provides a *Form* that uses the *Class*. It has a *LabelBox* (untouchable) for the balance, a *Textbox* for the amount, a *CheckBox* to determine whether the transaction is a deposit or withdrawal, and a *Button* to perform the transaction.

In order to open the *Form*, we could use an event – for instance, when *Sheet2* gets activated. Other ways of calling the *Form* are also valid, of course.

Table 69

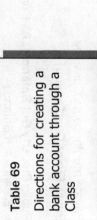

Directions for creating a bank account through a Class

Steps to Take – Creating a bank account

1. *Project → Add Class.*

2. Add your code to the Class (see below).

3. *Project → Add Windows Form.*

4. Drag onto the *Form*, from the *Common Controls*:
   A *LabelBox* (for the account balance), a *TextBox* (for the amount), a *CheckBox* (for deposit yes/no), and a *Button* (for the transaction).

5. Add code to their event handlers as we will do in the next Case Study (see below).

VBA Version

VSTO Version

Code Example 64: Building and Using a Class for Bank Transactions

'Class Module **Class1**

Private mBalance As Currency
Public **Event OverDrawn()**

Public Property Get **Balance**() As Currency
   Balance = mBalance
End Property

Public Property **Let Balance**(ByVal cBalance As Currency)
   mBalance = cBalance
End Property

Public Property Get TransTime() As Date 'Read-only
   TransTime = TimeValue(Now())
End Property

Public Sub Deposit(cAmount As Currency)
   mBalance = mBalance + cAmount
End Sub

Public Sub Draw(cAmount As Currency)
   If Balance > cAmount Then
     mBalance = mBalance - cAmount

Public Class **Class1**

Private mBalance As Decimal
Public **Event OverDrawn()**

Public Property **Balance**() As Decimal
   Get
     Balance = mBalance
   End Get
   Set(ByVal value As Decimal)
     mBalance = value
   End Set
End Property

Public **ReadOnly** Property TransTime() As Date
   Get
     TransTime = TimeValue(Now().ToString)
   End Get
End Property

Public Sub Deposit(ByVal cAmount As Decimal)
   mBalance = mBalance + cAmount
End Sub

Public Sub Draw(ByVal cAmount As Decimal)
   If Balance > cAmount Then
     mBalance = mBalance - cAmount

VBA Version	VSTO Version

`Else`
`    RaiseEvent OverDrawn`
`End If`
`End Sub`
 	
`Public Function ReturnInterest(fAPR As Single) As Currency`
`ReturnInterest = mBalance * fAPR`
`End Function`
 	
`Private Sub Class_Initialize() 'Like a constructor`
`mBalance = 25 'as a startup incentive`
`End Sub`
	`Else`
	`    RaiseEvent OverDrawn()`
	`End If`
	`End Sub`
	
	`Public Function ReturnInterest(ByVal fAPR As Single) As Decimal`
	`ReturnInterest = mBalance * CDec(fAPR)`
	`End Function`
	
	`Public Sub New() 'Acts like a constructor`
	`mBalance = 25 'as a startup incentive`
	`End Sub`
	
	`End Class`

`'In UserForm1`
 	
`Private WithEvents oAccount As Class1`
 	
`Private Sub UserForm_Initialize()`
 	
`ActiveBook.Sheets.Add`
 	
`Set oAccount = New Class1`
 	
`oAccount.Balance = GetSetting(ActiveWorkbook.Name, _`
`    "Acc", "Bal", 25)`
	`Public Class Form1`
	
	`Dim WithEvents oAccount As Class1`
	
	`Dim thisWB As Excel.Workbook = _`
	`    CType(Globals.ThisWorkbook, _ Excel.Workbook)`
	
	`Private Sub Form1_Load(ByVal sender As System.Object, ByVal _`
	`    e As System.EventArgs) Handles MyBase.Load`
	`Dim WS As Excel.Worksheet = _`
	`    CType(thisWB.Sheets.Add(), Excel.Worksheet)`
	`oAccount = New Class1`
	
	`Try`
	`    oAccount.Balance = CDec(GetSetting(thisWB.Name, _`
	`        "Acc", "Bal", "25"))`

From VBA to VSTO: Is Excel's New Engine for You?

VBA Version	VSTO Version

VBA Version

```
Label1.Caption = FormatCurrency(oAccount.Balance)
Textbox1 = 25
Checkbox1.Caption = "Deposit"
End Sub

Private Sub CommandButton1_Click()

Dim r As Integer, bAdd As Boolean

If TextBox1 = "" Then Exit Sub
If CheckBox1 = True Then
    oAccount.Deposit TextBox1
Else
    oAccount.Draw TextBox1
End If
If MsgBox("Add APR?", vbYesNo) = vbYes Then
    oAccount.Deposit oAccount.ReturnInterest(0.05)
    bAdd = True
End If
Label1 = FormatCurrency(oAccount.Balance)
With ActiveSheet.Range("A1").CurrentRegion
    r = .Rows.Count + 1
    .Cells(r, 1) = oAccount.TransTime
```

VSTO Version

```
Catch ex As Exception
    MsgBox("New Account with $25 incentive")
End Try
Label1.Text = FormatCurrency(oAccount.Balance)
TextBox1.Text = "25"
CheckBox1.Text = "Deposit"
End Sub

Private Sub Button1_Click(ByVal sender As Object, ByVal e _
    As System.EventArgs) Handles Button1.Click

Dim r As Integer, bAdd As Boolean
Dim WS As Excel.Worksheet = _
    CType (thisWB.Application.ActiveSheet, Excel.Worksheet)
Dim CR As Excel.Range = _
    CType(WS.Range("A1").CurrentRegion, Excel.Range)

If TextBox1.Text = "" Then Exit Sub
If CheckBox1.Checked = True Then
    oAccount.Deposit(CDec(TextBox1.Text))
Else
    oAccount.Draw(CDec(TextBox1.Text))
End If
If MsgBox("Add APR?", MsgBoxStyle.YesNo) = _
    MsgBoxResult.Yes Then
    oAccount.Deposit(oAccount.ReturnInterest(0.045))
    bAdd = True
End If
Label1.Text = FormatCurrency(oAccount.Balance)
WS.Activate()
r = CR.Rows.Count + 1
CR.Cells(r, 1) = oAccount.TransTime
```

VBA Version

```
If CheckBox1 = False Then
    .Cells(r , 2) = FormatCurrency(TextBox1)
Else
    .Cells(r , 3) = FormatCurrency(TextBox1)
End If
.Cells(r, 4) = FormatCurrency(oAccount.Balance)
If bAdd = True Then .Cells(r, 5) = "4.5%": bAdd = False
.EntireColumn.AutoFit
End With

End Sub

Private Sub UserForm_Terminate()

SaveSetting ActiveWorkbook.Name, "Acc", "Bal", _
    oAccount.Balance

End Sub

Private Sub oAccount_OverDrawn()
MsgBox "Account overdrawn; not allowed"
End Sub
```

VSTO Version

```
If CheckBox1.Checked = True Then
    CR.Cells(r, 2) = FormatCurrency(TextBox1.Text)
Else
    CR.Cells(r, 3) = FormatCurrency(TextBox1.Text)
End If
CR.Cells(r, 4) = FormatCurrency(oAccount.Balance)
If bAdd = True Then CR.Cells(r, 5) = "4.5%" : bAdd = False
CR.EntireColumn.AutoFit()
End Sub

Private Sub Form1_FormClosing(ByVal sender As Object, ByVal _
    e As System.Windows.Forms.FormClosingEventArgs) _
    Handles Me.FormClosing
    SaveSetting(thisWB.Name, "Acc", "Bal", _
        oAccount.Balance.ToString)

End Sub

Private Sub oAccount_OverDrawn() Handles oAccount.OverDrawn
MsgBox("Account overdrawn; not allowed")
End Sub

End Class
```

From VBA to VSTO: Is Excel's New Engine for You?

VBA Version

```
'In Module

Sub OpenBank()
    UserForm1.Show vbModal

End Sub
```

VSTO Version

```
Module myModule

    Sub OpenBank()
        Dim WF As Form1 = New Form1
        WF.ShowDialog()
    End Sub

End Module
```

12   Deployment and Security

12.1 Security

VBA used to work with Office macro security, which offers three different levels of security (high, medium, and low).

High **macro security level:**
No code would run unless you had digitally signed your code by using *selfcert.exe*, so the signed code would always be allowed to run.

Medium **macro security level:**
The user would decide whether to trust the VBA code imbedded into the *.xls* file.

Low **macro security level:**
Any code would run; however, by choosing this setting you would expose your computer to potentially malicious codes.

VSTO is a completely different ball game. It does not use Office macro security, but instead it employs several types of security evidence, such as *Application Directory* check, *Strong Name* assignment, *URL* verification, and so on. I won't go into all the details here.

Permission can be granted to various degrees. The most important ones for our immediate needs are these two:

FullTrust:
This permission set gives code unrestricted access to all protected resources; it allows full access to your computer's resources such as the file system or network access, potentially operating outside the control of the security system, which can be very risky.

Execution:
When this permission is given, assemblies can load and execute. If they try to do anything else (such as accessing a file), they will fail.

By default, Office won't load any assemblies, which means you cannot run any *.dll* file referenced by your Excel Workbook. The security system grants permission only if it is granted at four policy levels:

Enterprise level:
Default is *FullTrust* (to do anything the current user has authority to do).

Machine level:
Default is *NoTrust*, but there are three zones: local machine (*FullTrust*), internet and intranet (*PartialTrust*, which does not allow changes to files or to registry keys).

User level:
Default is *FullTrust*.

 Application level:
Default is *FullTrust*.

How come you were able to run all the assemblies we have created so far on your machine? The reason is rather simple: Since you created each assembly on your own machine, VSTO automatically adjusted permissions for you whenever you tested your code by hitting the *Debug* or *Build* button. But as soon as you reallocate the assembly to another location on your own machine, or when you give the assembly to other users (through copies, internet, or intranet), the assembly will not run! It must be made "trustworthy"; most of the time, this has to be done manually and one-by-one.

Where can you find the permissions VSTO has given to all the projects on your machine so far? They can be found in *.NET Framework 2.0 Configuration*.

Table 70	**Steps to Take – .NET Framework 2.0 Configuration**
Directions for locating and expanding the .NET Framework 2.0 Configuration	1. *Start → Control Panel.* 2. *Performance and Maintenance → Administrative Tools.* 3. Double-click *.NET Framework 2.0 Configuration.* 4. Expand the node of ⊕ *My Computer.* 5. Expand the node of ⊕ *Runtime Security Policy.* 6. Expand the node of ⊕ *User.* 7. Expand the node of ⊕ *Code Groups.* 8. Expand the node of ⊕ *All Code* (and perhaps drilling down further). 9. … until you see something like this:

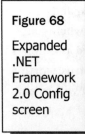

Figure 68

Expanded
.NET
Framework
2.0 Config
screen

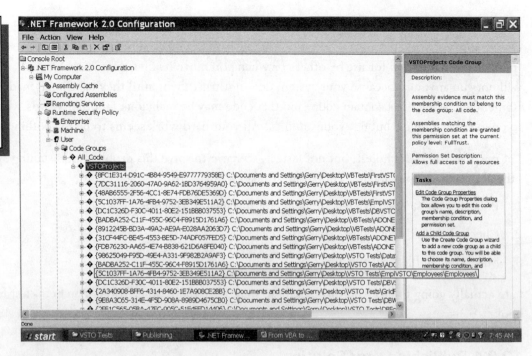

Each *Solution* you have tested on your machine has been given security permissions, especially as to its *.dll* files. And that's what you see listed in the previous screen under *All Code*. Microsoft's new security system is very involved and very versatile. In this book, I will simply focus on its basic structure – which is only the tip of the iceberg.

The structure of each section under *All Code* is basically like this:

> ➤ There is a main entry for each Solution. It has a key number assigned to it plus a URL to the Solution's main folder. Each main entry participates in the settings of the *All Code* section that it is under. There is no permission involved here.

> ➤ Then there is a sub-entry that provides *Execution* permission to all the files in a specific sub-folder.

> ➤ Finally, there is a sub-sub-entry that gives *FullTrust* permission to a specific assembly (*.dll*) inside the previous sub-folder.

Any assembly that is missing in this listing is considered "suspicious" and will not run. So what we need to do is to make a reallocated assembly "trusted" by adding it to this list. That will be the subject of the next few chapters.

12.2 Deployment

The code you write in VSTO is built as a *.dll* file. Consequently, it can be stored in any number of places – for instance, close to the document it is "linked" to, but also on a network share, on a corporate intranet, or on a secured internet site.

When you built your *Solution*, all files were neatly packed for you in folders and subfolders, and everything has worked properly ever since because VSTO made sure it would. However, when you "publish" your solution for use by others or when you move its files to another location, the assemblies will not run anymore because your system does not trust them until they have been made trustworthy. Remember, assemblies contain code, and that code may be malicious. In other words, you will be able to open your *.xls* files, but not your *.dll* files! All your hard work seems to be for nothing.

Let me give you the simplest, but not fastest, scenario to solve this problem of installing assemblies on other locations (deployment). This strategy takes a few steps:

1. Publish your *Solution* in a new folder – for instance, *c:\Publish*.

2. Check the "link" from your *.xls* file to the *.dll* file.

3. Make the *.dll* file "trustworthy."

I am actually going to take you through these steps. Are there other ways? You bet – but not for this book.

12.2.1 Publishing your Solution

In order to walk you through this process, we are going to create a new *Solution* with just very simple code – let's say, displaying a *MessageBox* when the *Workbook* opens. After testing the *Solution*, you only have a so-called *Debug* version. In addition, you need a *Release* version, or you could skip this step and create a *Published* version in a folder of your choice.

Table 71 Directions for creating a *Published* version of a *Solution*	Steps to Take – Publishing your Solution
	1. Create a new folder on your C-drive: *C:\Publish*.
	2. Start a new *Project* and call it: *Test*.
	3. Place code in *ThisWorkbook_Startup*: *MsgBox("Welcome")*.
	4. Run the code and watch the *MessageBox* pop up.
	5. Now save the *Solution* in your regular VSTO section.
	6. Then select from the menu: *Build → Publish Solution*.
	7. In the Wizard, specify a location for your application – in this case, *C:\Publish*. Make sure you *Browse* to that folder.
	8. Finally, go → *Finish*. Done!

Figure 69   Specifying a location for the *Published* version

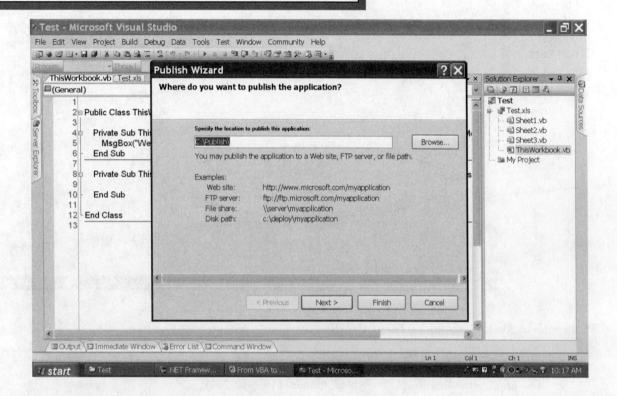

When you close VSTO and check the new location, you will see that it has a different structure this time.

This is the structure of the Publish folder.

➤ The Workbook   *Test.xls*

➤ The deployment manifest   *Test.application* (see 12.2.4)

➤ A separate subfolder   *Test_1.0.0.0*

The sub-folder has a so-called *version* number. Since this is the first release, it is numbered 1.0.0.0 (the next release will be *version* 1.0.0.1, which will be added as a second sub-folder, and so forth). Each time you create a new version of your *Solution*, you can regulate the new version number manually or automatically.

Project → Properties → Publish section *→ ☑ Automatically increment revision with each release*

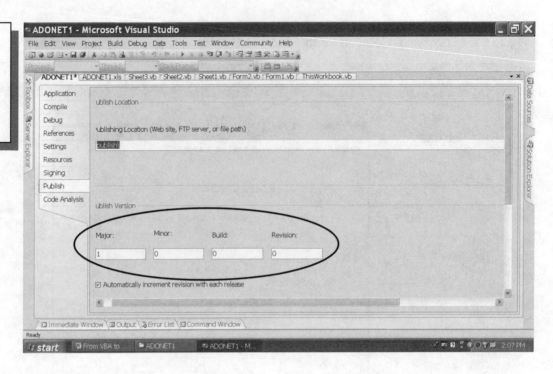

Figure 70

Managing release version numbers

So what's inside this sub-folder *Test_1.0.0.0*?

➤ The assembly   *Test.dll*

➤ The application manifest *Test.dll.manifest* (see 12.2.4)

➤ Copy of the Workbook   *Test.xls*

It all looks great, but you will experience quite a bummer when double-clicking the *.xls* file (either in the main folder or the subfolder)! The *.xls* file will open, but your *.dll* file will not.

12.2.2 Locating the Link Between .xls and .dll

Here is the error message you get when trying to run your Solution from the *.xls* file in the *Publish* folder. *The current .NET security policy does not permit the customization to run...*

Figure 71   The .Net Security system has not yet been notified of new permissions

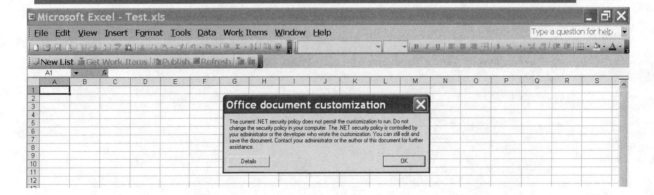

What we need to do is to find out where the link is between both files so we can make a copy of the assembly's key number.

<table>
<tr><td>

Table 72

Directions for locating link between .XLS and .DLL files

</td><td>

Locating and copying the link to the .dll file

1. Click *OK* on the error message you received.

2. Go: *File → Properties* (in Excel).

3. Select the *Custom* tab.

4. Click on the second Assembly property: *_AssemblyLocation*.

5. Notice its key value (a machine generated identifier).

6. Copy this key value (you need it for security settings).

</td></tr>
</table>

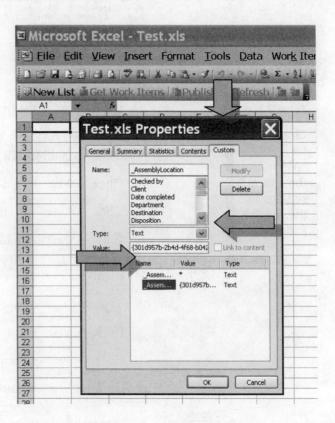

Figure 72

Locating link between .XLS and .DLL files

The Excel file "knows" where to find the *.dll* assembly that you want to run, but it is not allowed to access this file because it could harbor unsafe code. In other words, we have to mark the assembly as trusted. That is our third and last step.

12.2.3 Setting Security

As we saw before, Security settings are handled by *.NET Framework 2.0 Configuration* (see 12.1). It's there that we should create the three new settings for our *Publish* folder.

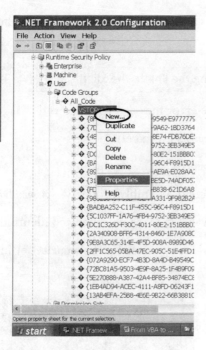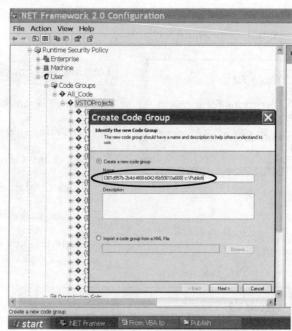

Figure 73
Creating new settings for the *Publish* folder

Table 73 Directions for creating three new settings for the *Publish* folder	**Main entry**	1. Right-click on the first group under *All Code → New*. 2. Paste the previously copied key number into the new code group name and add its URL: *C:\Publish*. 3. Click → *Next* → Condition Type: *All Code*. 4. Click → *Next* → Permission Set: **Nothing.** 5. Click → *Next* → *Finish*.
	Sub-entry	1. Right-click on the previous group → *New*. 2. Type any new code group name: *Test_1.0.0.0*. 3. Click → *Next* → Condition Type: *URL* → URL: *C:\Publish**. 4. Click → *Next* → Permission Set: **Execution.** 5. Click → *Next* → *Finish*.
	Sub-sub-entry	1. Right-click on the previous group → *New*. 2. Type any new code group name: *TestDLL*. 3. Click → *Next* → Condition Type: *URL* → URL: *C:\Publish\Test_1.0.0.0\Test.dll*. 4. Click → *Next* → Permission Set: **FullTrust.** 5. Click → *Next* → *Finish*.

After all of this is done, you should be able to run your assembly from either *.xls* file in your *Publish* folder. Your simple *MessageBox* should automatically pop up when you open the *WorkBook*! If not, you may have misspelled a small detail in any of the previous settings. Correct your mistakes until the assembly runs smoothly whenever you open the *.xls* file from the new location.

12.2.4 What are Manifests?

So far, we have seen two kinds of manifests: a *deployment* manifest and an *application* manifest. They were created by the *Publish Wizard*. You don't always need these manifests, but it may be helpful to know a little more about them – especially when you are moving things around.

It's easy to open and read a manifest. Just right-click on
Test.dll.manifest → Open With → NotePad.
NotePad shows you the content of this manifest

Tip:

Notice that file paths are hard-coded in this file. You can change things right here if you ever need to.

Figure 74   Viewing Manifest contents of first file in Notepad

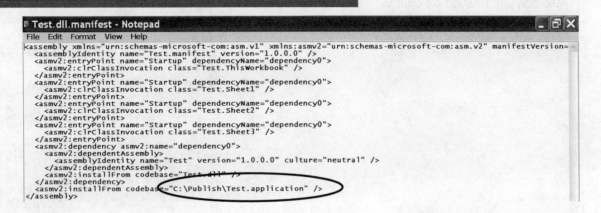

While still in the first file, you can open another one.
File → Open → folder Publish → file Test.application

Tip:

NotePad *gives you a look inside another file. This is very helpful if you need to change file paths some day, as is likely.*

Figure 75   Viewing Manifest contents of second file in Notepad

There is much more to the issue of deployment, especially in relation to deployment through intranet and internet. But that is far beyond the limited scope of this book.

You may even wish to create professional installers for your project – like those you have seen in professional applications. Such an aspiration calls for another *Project* inside your existing *Solution*: a so-called *Setup* project. All I will tell you here is how to get started. The rest is up to you.

Table 74

Directions for creating a Setup system

Steps to Take – Creating a Setup System

1. Add personal information to your project first.

2. Click *Project* → (Test) *Properties*.

3. Click *Application* tab → hit the button *Assembly Information*.

4. Adjust entries if you wish.

Figure 76   Making changes to entries in Assembly Information dialog box

Steps to Take – Creating a Setup System, cont.

5. Now start your *Setup* project next to your existing project inside your current *Solution*.
    Your *Solution* will now hold two projects.

6. Click *File* → *Add* → *New Project*.

7. Click *Project Types* → *Other Project Types* → *Deployment and Setup*.

8. Choose either *Setup Project* or *Setup Wizard* (the latter one takes you step by step).

9. Have a smooth trip!

13 Migrating from VBA to VSTO

13.1 VBA or VSTO?

Is your future going to be VBA or VSTO? If you have a choice – depending on your own situation, your company's decision, and Microsoft's policy – you may want to combine both tools, or you may settle on one of them. We report, you decide!

When is VBA your best bet?

➢ When you don't own or cannot afford *.NET*, its *Framework,* and all that comes with it.

➢ When you want to interact with applications other than Word and Excel.

➢ When your code needs to travel with the document.

➢ Or when you just want the simple syntax you are already used to!

When is VSTO your best bet?

➢ When you want easier code maintenance. Your assembly can be used by several documents and is physically detached from any document.

➢ When you desire easy extended functionality, such as creating reports, connecting to servers, etc.

➢ When you need a safer security model and a better way of deploying your code.

➢ When you need to protect your code from view and from inadvertent changes by non-professionals.

➢ When you want more powerful resources, such as Web services, Database connections, etc.

➢ When you crave a more consistent and powerful programming language, including interaction with other languages (used by yourself or your colleagues).

➢ When you work in a team with other programmers or developers.

13.2 Automatic and/or Manual Migration

As you have seen so far, there are many differences between VBA and VSTO – so don't expect a smooth ride when you want to cross the border between both territories. There is a lot of manual adjustment ahead of you, but fortunately also some automatic fixing. Let us break up the total problem into a few disparate issues:

➤ The good news is that you can just keep your existing Excel spreadsheets! Just take all VBA code out of the workbook (unless you want to maintain "old" macros as VBA macros) and save the emptied Excel workbook version under a new name. It can be used directly in your new *Solution*.

➤ The bad news is that you must redo all your *Form* related issues, because the differences between *UserForms* and *Windows.Forms* are more than minor.

➤ You can keep using your ADO management code based on the "old" ADO Library – albeit with a few adjustments. But you may decide to use ADO.NET instead – which requires more work but delivers better performance in return.

➤ Make a decision as to what to do with your old macros: Either you keep them in VBA or you transport them to VSTO (see 2.4).

➤ Then we have the code left that takes care of the ordinary business logic – mostly located in regular modules and class modules. The good news is here that there is some help around the corner: Move the module(s) from your original Workbook into your project and then get some help.

What help can you get in migrating your existing VBA code?

   You can use the *Upgrade Wizard* on exported VBA modules.

Table 75 Directions for using the Upgrade Wizard to migrate your code	**Steps to Take – VB 2005 Upgrade Wizard**
	1. Export the existing module(s) as a *.vbp* file.
	2. Add the exported code file to the project.
	3. Save and close the project.
	4. Open VS 2005: *File → Open → Convert*.
	5. Select the *VB 2005 Upgrade Wizard*.
	6. The Wizard creates a *.vb* file.
	7. Add this file to the VSTO project directory.
	8. Right-Click the project name → select *Add Existing →* select your *.vb* file.
	Now the migrated code is part of the project.

Note:

This Wizard is only available if you have *Visual Basic 6.0* on your machine.

You can also apply the executable *VBUpgrade.exe* using the *VBUpgrade FileName.vbp* command-line tool. (Make sure you have the right location: *C:\Program Files\ Microsoft Visual Studio 8\Vb\ VBUpgrade*).

 For a more limited portion of code, you can use the *Upgrade* tool.

Table 76

Directions for using the Upgrade tool to migrate your code

Steps to Take – Upgrade tool

1. Copy the VBA code onto the *Clipboard*.
2. In VSTO: *Tools → Upgrade VB 6.0 code*.
3. Paste the code into the dialog box.
4. Hit the *Upgrade* button.
5. Copy and paste the upgraded code into VSTO.

 Note:

Be aware that this is a rather limited option, because you can easily get error messages.

 Finally, there is the old-fashioned copy-and-paste method, which is usually your best bet.

Table 77

Directions for using copy-and-paste to migrate your code

Steps to Take – Copy-and-paste

1. Make sure you paste the old code into the correct section.
2. You will find all kinds of squiggles and wavy lines in the code to tell you where the problems are that need manual adjustment.
That's where you are going to need the previous chapters!

 Note:

The IDE will highlight the problem sections of your code and provide some helpful suggestions in the tooltip text.

13.3 Case Study: A Rosetta Stone

Figure 77

Transferring VBA code into VSTO

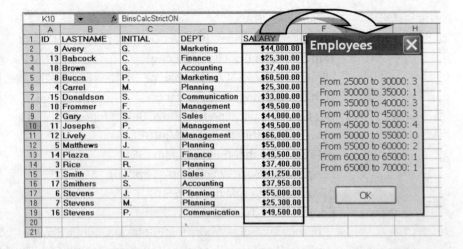

The following code starts from a selected range of numeric values and generates a frequency table based on these values.

It achieves this result by taking the following steps: It locates the minimum and maximum values, asks for an interval value, creates bins accordingly, and calculates the frequency for each bin. Most calculations are done via *WorksheetFunction*.

The code was originally made in VBA and then transferred to VSTO in several stages.

The code is really basic – without any validity checking or exception handling.

Code Example 65: Transferring VBA Code into VSTO

Original VBA code	

```
Sub BinsCalcVBA()
    Dim iStep As Integer, pMin As Double, pMax As Double
    Dim pStart As Double, I As Long
    Dim pFromBinsBot As Double, pFromBinsTop As Double, pInsideBin As Double
    Dim txt As String, SEL As Range
    Set SEL = Application.InputBox("Select Figures",,,,,,,8)
    pMin = WorksheetFunction.Min(SEL)
    pMax = WorksheetFunction.Max(SEL)
    iStep = InputBox("Which step?", , 5000)
    pStart = pMin - (pMin Mod iStep)
    For I = pStart To pMax Step iStep
        pFromBinsBot = WorksheetFunction.CountIf(SEL, ">=" & I)
        pFromBinsTop = WorksheetFunction.CountIf(SEL, ">=" & (I + iStep))
        pInsideBin = pFromBinsBot - pFromBinsTop
        txt = txt & vbCr & "From " & I & " to " & (I + iStep) & ": " & pInsideBin
    Next I
    MsgBox txt
End Sub
```

Copied into VSTO with Strict OFF

```
1  Option Strict Off
2
3  Module Module1
4
5      Sub BinsCalcVBA()
6          Dim iStep As Integer, pMin As Double, pMax As Double
7          Dim pStart As Double, I As Long
8          Dim pFromBinsBot As Double, pFromBinsTop As Double, pInsideBin As Double
9          Dim txt As String, SEL As Range
10         SEL = Application.InputBox("Select Figures", , , , , , , 8)
11         pMin = WorksheetFunction.Min(SEL)
12         pMax = WorksheetFunction.Max(SEL)
13         iStep = InputBox("Which step?", , 5000)
14         pStart = pMin - (pMin Mod iStep)
15         For I = pStart To pMax Step iStep
16             pFromBinsBot = WorksheetFunction.CountIf(SEL, ">=" & I)
17             pFromBinsTop = WorksheetFunction.CountIf(SEL, ">=" & (I + iStep))
18             pInsideBin = pFromBinsBot - pFromBinsTop
19             txt = txt & vbCr & "From " & I & " to " & (I + iStep) & ": " & pInsideBin
20         Next I
21         MsgBox(txt)
22     End Sub
23
24  End Module
```

Fixed with Strict OFF	Option Strict **Off**

Module Module1

Dim thisWB As Excel.Workbook = CType(Globals.ThisWorkbook, Excel.Workbook)

```
Sub BinsCalcVBA()
    Dim iStep As Integer, pMin As Double, pMax As Double
    Dim pStart As Double, I As Long
    Dim pFromBinsBot As Double, pFromBinsTop As Double, pInsideBin As Double
    Dim txt As String = "", SEL As Excel.Range
    SEL = thisWB.Application.InputBox("Select Figures", , , , , , , 8)
    pMin = thisWB.Application.WorksheetFunction.Min(SEL)
    pMax = thisWB.Application.WorksheetFunction.Max(SEL)
    iStep = InputBox("Which step?", , 5000)
    pStart = pMin - (pMin Mod iStep)
    For I = pStart To pMax Step iStep
        pFromBinsBot = thisWB.Application.WorksheetFunction.CountIf(SEL, ">=" & I)
        pFromBinsTop = thisWB.Application.WorksheetFunction.CountIf(SEL, ">=" & _
            (I + iStep))
        pInsideBin = pFromBinsBot - pFromBinsTop
        txt = txt & vbCr & "From " & I & " to " & (I + iStep) & ": " & pInsideBin
    Next I
    MsgBox(txt)
End Sub
```

End Module |
| **Copied from Strict OFF to Strict ON** | ```
1   Option Strict On
2
3   Module Module3
4
5       Dim thisWB As Excel.Workbook = CType(Globals.ThisWorkbook, Excel.Workbook)
6
7       Sub BinsCalcVBA()
8           Dim iStep As Integer, pMin As Double, pMax As Double
9           Dim pStart As Double, I As Long
10          Dim pFromBinsBot As Double, pFromBinsTop As Double, pInsideBin As Double
11          Dim txt As String = "", SEL As Excel.Range
12          SEL = thisWB.Application.InputBox("Select Figures", , , , , , , 8)
13          pMin = thisWB.Application.WorksheetFunction.Min(SEL)
14          pMax = thisWB.Application.WorksheetFunction.Max(SEL)
15          iStep = InputBox("Which step?", , 5000)
16          pStart = pMin - (pMin Mod iStep)
17          For I = pStart To pMax Step iStep
18              pFromBinsBot = thisWB.Application.WorksheetFunction.CountIf(SEL, ">=" & I)
19              pFromBinsTop = thisWB.Application.WorksheetFunction.CountIf(SEL, ">=" & (I + iStep))
20              pInsideBin = pFromBinsBot - pFromBinsTop
21              txt = txt & vbCr & "From " & I & " to " & (I + iStep) & ": " & pInsideBin
22          Next I
23          MsgBox(txt)
24      End Sub
``` |
```

Fixed with Strict ON	Option Strict **On**
	
	Module Module2
	
	   Dim thisWB As Excel.Workbook = CType(Globals.ThisWorkbook, Excel.Workbook)
	
	   Sub BinsCalcVBA()
	     Dim iStep As Integer, pMin As Double, pMax As Double
	     Dim pStart As Double, I As Long
	     Dim pFromBinsBot As Double, pFromBinsTop As Double, pInsideBin As Double
	     Dim txt As String = "", SEL As Excel.Range
	     SEL = **CType(**thisWB.Application.InputBox("Select Figures", , , , , , , 8)**, _**
	       Excel.Range)
	     pMin = thisWB.Application.WorksheetFunction.Min(SEL)
	     pMax = thisWB.Application.WorksheetFunction.Max(SEL)
	     iStep = **CInt(**InputBox("Which step?", , **"5000")**)
	     pStart = pMin - (pMin Mod iStep)
	     For I = **CLng(**pStart**)** To **CLng(**pMax**)** Step iStep
	       pFromBinsBot = thisWB.Application.WorksheetFunction.CountIf(SEL, ">=" & I)
	       pFromBinsTop = thisWB.Application.WorksheetFunction.CountIf(SEL, ">=" & _
	         (I + iStep))
	       pInsideBin = pFromBinsBot - pFromBinsTop
	       txt = txt & vbCr & "From " & I & " to " & (I + iStep) & ": " & pInsideBin
	     Next I
	     MsgBox(txt)
	   End Sub
	
	End Module

14   What Do You Need to Get Started?

14.1 How, What, and When to Install

Before you get started, check whether you have the correct hardware and system requirements.

Table 78

Minimum hardware and system requirements

Device	Requirements
Processor	766 MHz (preferably 1.5 GHz)
RAM	256 MB (preferably 512 MB)
Hard Disk space	1.5 GB on system drive 4.5 GB on installation drive
Operating System	Windows 2000 (Professional)

In order to use VSTO, the following software and components must be installed on your computer:

- *MS Visual Studio .NET* (2003+; or *Standard* 2003+; build 3077+).
  Do this before installing MS Office!

- *MS Office Professional* 2003+ edition (or just *MS Office Excel* 2003+).
  You do need more than a *Standard* installation; best is a *Full* installation, or at least the following components:

- Make sure *Service Pack 1* (SP1) is included. Otherwise, download it from www.microsoft.com.

- Install also VBA and *the .NET programmability support*. The latter will put the *Primary Interop Assemblies* (*PIAs*) on your machine (in the *Windows Global Assembly Cache*, or GAC, created by the *.NET Framework*) – with the option "Run From My Computer". Make sure you have PIAs for at least Excel, MSForms, and Graph. These PIAs are the "connection" between VS.NET and your Office applications.

- Finally, install VSTO as the crowning glory. *The Team Suite* CD is minimal, but sufficient.

- You may also want to also install *MS SQL Server* or *MS SQL Server Desktop Engine* (MSDE 7.0+ or 2000+) if you need to connect Excel to an SQL server for database purposes. MSDE is included with your Office 2003 CD.

- One more caveat: Your monitor should **not** be set to *High Contrast*.
  To fix this: *Control Panel* → *Accessibility Options* → *Display* → □ *Use High Contrast*.
  If you do have to change the *Contrast* setting, you must run the setup for VSTO again.

After this installation, you will find new additional choices in the *New Project* dialog box of *Visual Studio* 2003+: There is a new node called *MS Office System projects*. Pick your favorite language – probably VB.NET – and start a VSTO Excel project, after you have decided on the question as to whether you wish to create a companion document or to attach this assembly to an existing Excel document.

People who want to use your *.dll* files newly created in VSTO on their own computers are called *End Users*. What should be installed on their computers?

🐧 *MS .NET Framework* version 2.0+ (before installing Office 2003+).

🐧 VSTO runtime (a mini version of VSTO).

🐧 *MS Office Professional* 2003+ (or at least MS Office Excel 2003+), including the necessary *Primary Interop Assemblies* (PIAs).

🐧 Make sure Office 2003+ *Service Pack* (SP1) was also included. If not, you can still download it from www.microsoft.com.

14.2 Useful Resources

Microsoft Resources	
www.windowsforms.net	msdn.microsoft.com/msdnmag/
www.microsoft.com/vsnet/tools/office	msdn.microsoft.com/netframework
	msdn.microsoft.com/library/techart/
	msdn.microsoft.com/newsgroups
msdn.microsoft.com/vstudio/tryit/	msdn2.microsoft.com/en-us/library
msdn.microsoft.com/library/en-us/	
msdn.microsoft.com/office/	
Other Resources	
www.devx.com/codemag	www.codeguru.com/
www.devx.com/officeprodev	www.gotdotnet.com
www.devx.com/dotnet	dotnet.sys-con.com/

14.3 Are You Ready?

Well, that's about it – you've got the information, the rationale, and the examples you need to get started in VSTO. The rest is up to you. We provide, you decide …

Index

HOLY MACRO! BOOKS QUICK ORDER FORM

Fax Orders: (707)-220-4510. Send this form.
E-Mail Orders: store@MrExcel.com - Online: http://www.MrExcel.com
Postal Orders: MrExcel, 13386 Judy Ave NW, PO Box 82, Uniontown OH 44685, USA

Quantity	Title	Price	Total
	Learn Excel from Mr Excel By Bill Jelen ISBN 1-932802-12-6 (853 pages – 2005)	$39.95	
	Excel for Teachers By Conmy, Hazlett, Jelen, Soucy ISBN 1-932802-11-8 (236 pages – 2006)	$24.95	
	Excel for Marketing Managers By Bill Jelen and Ivana Taylor ISBN 1-932802-13-4 (172 Pages – 2006)	$24.95	
	Office VBA Macros You Can Use Today By Gonzales et al ISBN 1-932802-06-1 (433 Pages – 2006)	$39.95	
	Holy Macro! It's 2,200 Excel VBA Examples (CD-ROM) By Hans Herber Bill Jelen and Tom Urtis ISBN 1-932802-08-8 (2200 pages – 2004)	$89.00	
	FromVBA to VSTO: Is Excel's New engine for You? By Dr. Gerard Verschuuren ISBN 1-932802-14-2 (200 pages – 2006)	$29.95	
	Slide Your Way Through Excel VBA (CD-ROM) By Dr. Gerard Verschuuren ISBN 0-9724258-6-1 (734 pages – 2003)	$99.00	
	Join the Excellers League (CD-ROM) By Dr. Gerard Verschuuren ISBN 1-932802-00-2 (1477 pages – 2004)	$99.00	
	Excel for Scientists (CD-ROM) By Dr. Gerard Verschuuren ISBN 0-9724258-8-8 (589 pages – 2004)	$75.00	
	Guerilla Data Analysis Using Microsoft Excel By Bill Jelen ISBN 0-9724258-0-2 (138 pages – 2002)	$19.95	
	The Spreadsheet at 25 By Bill Jelen ISBN 1-932802-04-5 (120 color pages – 2005)	$19.95	
	Grover Park George On Access By George Hepworth ISBN 0-9724258-9-6 (480 pages – 2004)	$29.95	
	Your Access to the World (CD-ROM) By Dr. Gerard Verschuuren ISBN 1-932802-03-7 (1450 pages – 2004)	$99.00	
	Access VBA Made Accessible (CD-ROM) By Dr. Gerard Verschuuren (1323 pages – 2004)	$99.00	
	DreamBoat On Word By Anne Troy ISBN 0-9724258-4-5 (220 pages – 2004)	$19.95	
	Kathy Jacobs On PowerPoint By Kathy Jacobs ISBN 0-9724258-6-1 (380 pages – 2004)	$29.95	
	Unleash the Power of Outlook 2003 By Steve Link ISBN 1-932802-01-0 (250 pages – 2004)	$19.95	
	Unleash the Power of OneNote By Kathy Jacobs & Bill Jelen (320 pages – 2004)	$19.95	
	VBA and Macros for Microsoft Excel By Bill Jelen and Tracy Syrstad ISBN 0789731290 (576 Pages – 2004)	$39.95	
	Pivot Table Data Crunching By Bill Jelen and Michael Alexander ISBN 0789734354 (275 Pages – 2005)	$29.95	

Name: _____

Address: _____

City, State, Zip: _____

E-Mail: _____

Sales Tax: Ohio residents add 6% sales tax

Shipping by Air: **US:** $4 for first book, $2 per additional book. $1 per CD.

                    International: $9 for first book, $5 per additional book. $2 per CD

                    FedEx available on request at actual shipping cost.

Payment: Check or Money order to "MrExcel" or pay with VISA/MC/Discover/AmEx:

                    Card #:_____ Exp.:_____

                    Name on Card: _____

Bulk Orders: Ordering enough for the entire staff? Save 40% when you order six or more of any one title.